Ducks in the Median:

6 Parables on how to live on the other side our our rescue

By Dr. Tim Farrell

Ducks in the Median

6 parables on how to live on the other side of our rescue

© 2010 by Tim Farrell

All rights reserved. Except for brief exceprts for review and portions where duplicating permission is specifically granted, no part of this book may be reproduced or transmitted in any way without written permission from the author. For permission, email: TimFarrell@ucumc.net.

Printed by Lulu Press. For additional copies: http://www.lulu.com

Cover and Interior Design: Carolyn B. Smith

Scripture quotations, unless otherwise noted, are taken from the Holy Bible, New Living Translation, copyright ©1996, 2004, 2007. Used by permission of Tyndale House Publishers, Inc., Carol Stream, Illinois 60188. All rights reserved.

ISBN: 978-0-557-63320-3

FOR...

TRACEY—The love of my life.

CHATHAM and MOLLY—The joys of my heart.

Contents

Introduction vii

Parable 1: Ducks in the Median

    Rescued into a Life of Gratitude 9

Parable 2: Wheat-Cracker and Jelly-Bean Sandwiches

    Rescued into a Life of Obedience 45

Parable 3: Four-Eyed Gator

    Rescued into a Life of Relinquishment 71

Parable 5: Bus 90

    Rescued into a Life of Courage 97

Parable 5: Sweaty Starfish

    Rescued into a Life of Preparedness 133

Parable 6: White Canvas High Tops

    Rescued into a Life of Community 163

Conclusion 189

Thanks to...

Jesus—the one who's rescued me and reminded me that, in the midst of weakness, there is the weight and power of his strength. All glory to him who has reached out to all of creation with the purpose of leading us into a life of gratitude and godliness.

Tracey—my wife, who encouraged me to be myself in the writing process. I love you; you're my best friend and I'm grafeful that you're in my life.

Chatham and Molly—our kids, who always gave encouragement and showed interest in the many silly memories I shared in the book. You both are the best!

Ed and Judy Kelley—my mother- and father-in-law, for their prayers, encouragement and help in shaping me. Thank you.

Pastor Joe MacLaren—for his willingness to give me the time to write, for the encouragement that I could see this project all the way through, and for his friendship. I'm grateful for you.

University Carillon United Methodist Church—for the staff and the people of the church who encouraged me and put up with my antics.

Carolyn Smith—for her insight and help in designing and making the printed page reflect what we envisioned.

Steve Brooks and Andy Lowry—for their friendship and commitment to Jesus. I love and respect who you are.

Mom, Mike and Matt—Thank you for helping me to grow up in a God-honoring home.

Introduction

Oswald Chambers said, "The saint who satisfies the heart of Jesus will make other saints strong and mature for God."[1] In writing this book and curriculum, I believe I am satisfying the heart of Jesus. Both my kids and my wife have noticed the grey hairs increasing and the hairline receding and in convicted unison have urged me to "step it up" and actually write a discipleship curriculum. So here I am, squeezed into the masses of other voices and writers not so sure if I'm being a fool for the Lord or simply a fool. But I believe this is pleasing to the heart of Jesus because in one way or another, he's made me for this (or this for me). I offer it humbly to you.

Enclosed are simple and plain experiences from a simple and plain life. It's the way I see things and I hope it encourages you to see similar things in your own unique and creative way. I am convinced that all of life is a gift from the Father and as such, ALL OF IT—from the smooth-sailing plans for the week to the multiple and frustrating interruptions—can help us be formed into the likeness of Jesus our Lord. So in pleasing Jesus by fulfilling who he's made me to be, I am also banking on the hope of strength and maturity inundating your life. For you are something you might not want to say you are; you are a saint, and Jesus wants you to fulfill who he made you to be.

A saint is a person who is called to bring honor and glory to Jesus. The writers of the New Testament often referred to the recipients of their discourses as saints. There were no punches pulled. There were no timid allusions made or clues dropped. The plain fact of the matter was freely owned by the Apostles as well as the people who were the recipients of their ministries. Nothing has changed in the last 2,000 years. In Christ, you and I are saints. It's certainly nothing to brag about (pride and competition are antithetical to the way of Jesus), but it does mean something. What it means is the subject of this study.

---

1   Oswald Chambers, *My Utmost for His Highest*. Westwood, NJ: Barbour and Company Inc., 1963, 163.

Parable 1

Ducks in the Median:
Rescued into a Life of Gratitude

It was a busy Tuesday morning in Central Florida. We were up at 7 a.m. and Chatham and Molly needed to be to their school by a quarter after 8. After rubbing the sleep out of my eyes with a few cups of coffee, Tracey and I heard the kids stirring in their beds. Chatham dragged his Florida Gator pajama butt out of bed and collapsed on the TV-room couch. He caught a few more moments of sleep while we began to make his favorite breakfast: a homemade Egg McMuffin.

The sound of breaking eggs must have reached Molly because she rolled out of bed and walked into the kitchen with her eyes barely opened. Her black strands of long wispy hair, snarled and curled in a fantastic fabric of cuteness, reflected the deep sleep she had enjoyed and her disappointment with going back to school after a tiring Monday. Dragging her princess blanket behind her, Molly made her way to the love seat where she sat in hungry anticipation. A heaping bowl of *snap, crackle and pop* was served, and she woke up fully to the sounds of her own crunching and munching.

Like most every family, our kids have tasks they've got to get done before heading out the door to school. So they made their beds and put their clothes and shoes on. They brushed their hair and teeth. Chatham put the dog outside. Molly kept the cat inside. Doors were finally locked and we headed out to the van.

~ ~ ~ ~ ~

The kids' school is only a five-minute drive up the street, so most mornings are a quick and easy trip for us. But on this particular morning something caught my eye. A small flash of fluffy yellow plush blurred past as we drove up to the school. Not thinking much of it, we waded into line, dropped our kids off, and headed back home to get ready for work.

We were almost home when the same thing caught my eye again. It was down on my driver's side next to the well-manicured median. Although there was a lot of traffic, I took a moment to follow my peripheral vision and there it was … coming into focus: a small helpless duckling lying on its back with webbed feet sticking straight up into the air.

"Tracey! I think I just saw a little duckling stuck on its back!"

"Why don't you pull over and stop?" Tracey said.

"Can't!" I shot back. "I've got a meeting at church this morning."

As we pulled into our driveway, a rising conviction began to invade my mind. I couldn't help but think of the book we had read to Molly several times just the week before.

~ ~ ~ ~ ~

Make Way for Ducklings[1] is one of Molly's favorite children's books. It had been given to Molly when she was just a toddler, but she often returns to its penciled drawings of Boston and the award-winning story of how a family of ducks bravely makes their way through the city's busy streets.

Molly loves one picture in particular. It's the drawing of a stout Boston police officer. With eyebrows raised, baton in hand and whistle in mouth, he singlehandedly stops traffic to make a way for the ducklings. Molly often comments on how nice the officer is. She likes him a lot and is 100 percent sure her daddy loves little ducklings just as much.

Knowing this, I found myself not able to let the thought of the helpless duckling go. I looked at the clock. I glanced at the 3G phone. I double checked the calendar. I was reminded of the tight schedule on Tuesdays. But in the midst of all of the "no's" and the "I don't have times," the need to live up to my daughter's expectation of any Boston police officer (and loving father) grew inside of me.

"Tracey," I spoke loud enough so she could hear me in the bathroom where she was getting ready for work. "I'm just going to run up the street and see if the duckling is still there. I'll be back in a few minutes."

"OK, babe," Tracey replied.

I hopped back in the van, wondering what I was getting myself into. "I'm sure someone's already stopped and helped the little thing," I muttered softly to myself.

~ ~ ~ ~ ~

I pulled out of our subdivision and headed back up the street. As I arrived at the median where I had first spotted the bird, I was surprised to find it was still there. Only this time it was off of its back and running along the curbside median with cars whirring past it. Putting all pride aside I jumped out of the car and began jogging to the helpless bird (I was still decked out in a t-shirt, Superman pajama pants and green Crocs). I felt like I was in a slow-motion reunion you might watch on the silver screen. As I got closer to the duckling, I assumed it would be glad to see me. I couldn't have been more off the mark! It was terrified of me, and so its little legs dodged my grasp and led it into the path of oncoming traffic.

It quacked and I screamed. Fortunately, I was able to get a hold of its tiny backside as I scooped the duckling into my hand. With passing drivers staring at me, I stood there next to the median wondering what in the world I should do next. The duckling shivered in my hand. It was so small and helpless. It began to quack.

~ ~ ~ ~ ~

I decided to look for its mother. Thinking back to my daughter's book, I couldn't help but picture a mama duck and entourage of siblings. Nothing in the median. I sprinted across the street and canvassed the retention ponds. *How fast can ducks run? This is ridiculous!*

Pond after pond turned up empty. But then I spotted a large pond closer to the school. "Ducks!" I began to run toward it, all the while hoping and praying the duckling wouldn't take a poop in my hand. Yet, as I closed in on the pond-dwelling mallards, they must have caught wind of my pre-showered b.o., because they simply flew to the other side of the water.

I don't see little siblings ... It can't be them. You've gotta be kidding me!

After about thirty minutes of looking and searching, I gave up. I got back into the van and, as I held the duck in one hand and drove with the other, I found myself singing to the lost bird: "Hush little birdie don't say a word, papa's gonna buy you a..." I made up lyrics as I drove along. Arriving back at home, I walked into the bathroom where Tracey was finishing her shower.

"So, did you find the duckling?" she asked.

I didn't have to say a word. The bird did the talking for me.

~ ~ ~ ~

"Do you think ducklings make good pets?" I asked. One look at our curious tabby cat checked my impromptu plans. "This isn't going to work, is it?"

We tried calling the nearest animal hospital, but the hour was still early. Just an answering machine. "What are we going to do?" I stammered.

After dumping out Molly's Halloween candy and making a makeshift bed in the small pumpkin, Tracey and I began to brainstorm scenarios.

After some time of discussion we came up with a decision. "How about we give it one more shot and see if we can find the baby's mama?" Tracey said.

I was irritated and annoyed that this had cut into our working hours at church, but agreed that it'd be best to give it one more try.

~ ~ ~ ~

I've never tried shifting a vehicle from "D" to "P" while doing 15 mph, but the moment we saw her that's just what I did. The noise wasn't pleasant but the sensation of spotting both mama and her brood of ducklings was.

"There they are!" I shouted.

Mama mallard and her dozen babies were in the very same median where the rescue had taken place earlier that morning. I hadn't been able to see them because they were hidden deep in the midst of the bushes that dotted the landscaped center of the median.

Without thinking, I dodged the oncoming traffic and carried the lost duck right over to the median. I assumed mama would be tickled pink (or in this case, emerald green) to see her lost baby. Her baker's dozen of children would be complete, and surely this would be cause for joy. As I got closer to mama mallard and her babies, they all began to panic, quack and run in every direction imaginable. Some ran to nearby bushes while others flopped off the median into the paved roadway where the morning's rush hour traffic continued.

I was beside myself.

~ ~ ~ ~ ~

I was about to give up when I heard Tracey say, "Tim, try to get that jogger's attention over there on the sidewalk. Maybe he can help us!"

Approaching us from the left was a well-tanned and muscular jogger. His shirt must have long-since stopped wicking away sweat, as he was covered in perspiration. I called out, "Hey, Mr. Jogging Man! Can you help?"

Looking through polarized lenses he smiled and replied in a rather thick southern drawl, "What'cha doin'?"

Making quick footwork, he ran through the traffic to where we stood in the median.

"We're trying to get these ducks across the street safely. It looks like there's a mom duck and about thirteen little ones." I pointed all around us into the bracken of the bushes where the ducklings hid from view.

Without missing a step the man jogged in place as I explained all that had happened that morning. With a smile and a desire to take on the challenge, he said he'd be happy to help. Jogging all the while, he reached into bush after bush and began to help scoop up petrified quacking balls of fur. In Boston police posture, we each took turns stopping traffic as scared bundles of nerves were carried across the street and into the nearby woods. (We could only manage to pick them up one-by-one.) Mama duck was hardest of all. She ran and ducked (no pun intended). She hollered and nipped. Finally, we chased her waddling body across the street where she reunited with her babies.

On one occasion, the Good Samaritan who helped us leaped into the road, trying to snatch up a fugitive duckling. A passing motorist came just inches from hitting the man! I was amazed. A complete stranger joining us to help make a way for these ducklings, putting his life at risk to make sure that not one duck was lost or hurt.

Finally, after about three quarters of an hour of chasing and flagging down cars, all the ducks... every last one of them... were rescued and off and away into the safety of the woods. We thanked the man who had helped us and got back into the van and went to work.

As Tracey and I drove along, we couldn't help but smile and talk in excited tones. We relished the opportunity to tell our children about the rescue operation we had conducted. We knew they would be pleased with their parents and our joining the ranks of those who have made a way for ducklings.

~ ~ ~ ~ ~

As the day went on, I found myself looking out of my church study into the big Florida sky and wondering if the ducks we saved were grateful. They had been completely helpless and in their weakness we had been strong for them. Would they remember what we had done? Would it make a difference in how they would live?

~ ~ ~ ~ ~

If those ducks are anything like my dog, Lucy, they have less than a three-minute short-term memory bank. So, although they've been rescued, chances are pretty good they will go on to live normal mallard lives. But we're different. We do have memories that can last a lifetime. Further, what differentiates us from the rest of creation is our God-given ability to go beyond ourselves and to worship in response to what's been done on our behalf. In this urge to worship the Lord who has rescued us, I'm convinced the core conviction we need to rehearse on a daily basis is not only how Jesus has rescued us, but what this rescue means in terms of how we live on the other side of it.

This conviction comprises ALL of Jesus' teachings and commands. The way of life Jesus described, to those who were willing to listen and receive, was the kind of life he desired for all people to live into on the other side of their rescues. Taking this a step further, the vast bulk of the New Testament is comprised of counsel and letters from followers of Jesus who were doing their level best to remind, correct, protect and encourage the people who had been rescued on how to keep out of the medians around them and how to stay true to Jesus who had saved them.

What follows here—six weeks' worth—can be looked at as my best effort to help and encourage you in your life with Jesus. I'm using my own parables to springboard into the biblical material. Jesus often taught in parables. A parable is a short and simple story intended to illustrate an important lesson. Typically these kinds of stories come out of daily experiences, so there's nothing fancy or intellectual about them. I think that's a good thing, because life is made up of ordinary things.

Now hear me out. You may be in the thick of whatever median you're in, and you've never once allowed yourself to be rescued by Jesus. If this is the case for you, I hope this material helps you to realize how much Jesus loves you. I also hope that these readings will give you a small window into what life might look like if you do decide to waddle after him.

For those who have placed their trust in Jesus and consider him to be their Savior, I hope this material brings to mind the need to be concerned about how life is lived in response to all that Jesus has done, is doing, and will most certainly continue to do. I have purposefully set out the material in the manner that's before you, believing that each week builds on the previous one. Out of all the weeks, I'd say week 6 has a somewhat different tone and purpose. The community of faith is where we are to live each and every day, so it's not a culmination of what we'll be learning so much as an ongoing reality. Nevertheless, most people could take or leave the church in today's culture. Community has sadly become quite optional for many of us. So, given the difficult nature of the subject, I wanted to wait 'til the end to address it. You'll notice that a lot of this week's material reflects the concerns and frustrations of a pastor who's experienced the fickle attitudes of folks who come and go at whim. I hope you'll bear with me and understand that what I convey is out of both love for the individual and concern for the community God has created and called us to be faithful to.

At the end of each day there is a parable principle (the core truth coming out of that day's material), a scripture memory verse for that particular week, questions for reflection, and ideas on how to take what you're learning and processing and apply it to your life. I hope that each of these resources will better enable you to grab a hold of the material rather than let it roll off of your back. (Sorry... can't get ducks off the brain.) These resources are central to this journey and without them this becomes just another book, so I hope you'll utilize them fully.

BIBLICAL TEXT FOR WEEK 1: JOHN 21:1–23

John chapter 21 is my favorite account in the entire Bible. I guess it's because I find in Peter a guy I can relate to, and I see in Jesus the rescuing solace of a Savior who helps calm my own fears.

> A hint about reading the Bible: It's always good to read a passage in its entirety a couple of times through. Take in the overarching contour and context of the passage. Then go back and spend time looking at the account piece by piece, mulling over and prayerfully sifting through the verses.

1 Later, Jesus appeared again to the disciples beside the Sea of Galilee. This is how it happened. 2 Several of the disciples were there—Simon Peter, Thomas (nicknamed the Twin), Nathanael from Cana in Galilee, the sons of Zebedee, and two other disciples.

3 Simon Peter said, "I'm going fishing."

"We'll come, too," they all said. So they went out in the boat, but they caught nothing all night.

4 At dawn Jesus was standing on the beach, but the disciples couldn't see who he was. 5 He called out, "Fellows, have you caught any fish?"

"No," they replied.

6 Then he said, "Throw out your net on the right-hand side of the boat, and you'll get some!" So they did, and they couldn't haul in the net because there were so many fish in it.

7 Then the disciple Jesus loved said to Peter, "It's the Lord!" When Simon Peter heard that it was the Lord, he put on his tunic (for he had stripped for work), jumped into the water, and headed to shore. 8 The others stayed with the boat and pulled the loaded net to the shore, for they were only about a hundred yards from shore. 9 When they got there, they found breakfast waiting for them—fish cooking over a charcoal fire, and some bread.

10 "Bring some of the fish you've just caught," Jesus said. 11 So Simon Peter went aboard and dragged the net to the shore. There were 153 large fish, and yet the net hadn't torn.

12 "Now come and have some breakfast!" Jesus said. None of the disciples dared to ask him, "Who are you?" They knew it was the Lord. 13 Then Jesus served them the bread and the fish. 14 This was the third time Jesus had appeared to his disciples since he had been raised from the dead.

15 After breakfast Jesus asked Simon Peter, "Simon son of John, do you love me more than these?"

"Yes, Lord," Peter replied, "you know I love you."

"Then feed my lambs," Jesus told him.

16 Jesus repeated the question: "Simon son of John, do you love me?"

"Yes, Lord," Peter said, "you know I love you."

"Then take care of my sheep," Jesus said.

17 A third time he asked him, "Simon son of John, do you love me?"

Peter was hurt that Jesus asked the question a third time. He said, "Lord, you know everything. You know that I love you."

Jesus said, "Then feed my sheep.

18 "I tell you the truth, when you were young, you were able to do as you liked; you dressed yourself and went wherever you wanted to go. But when you are old, you will stretch out your hands, and others will dress you and take you where you don't want to go." 19 Jesus said this to let him know by what kind of death he would glorify God. Then Jesus told him, "Follow me."

20 Peter turned around and saw behind them the disciple Jesus loved—the one who had leaned over to Jesus during supper and asked, "Lord, who will betray you?" 21 Peter asked Jesus, "What about him, Lord?"

22 Jesus replied, "If I want him to remain alive until I return, what is that to you? As for you, follow me." 23 So the rumor spread among the community of believers that this disciple wouldn't die. But that isn't what Jesus said at all. He only said, "If I want him to remain alive until I return, what is that to you?"

Day 1: "Out of the Median of Fear"

1 Later, Jesus appeared again to the disciples beside the Sea of Galilee. This is how it happened. 2 Several of the disciples were there—Simon Peter, Thomas (nicknamed the Twin), Nathanael from Cana in Galilee, the sons of Zebedee, and two other disciples.

3 Simon Peter said, "I'm going fishing."

"We'll come, too," they all said. So they went out in the boat, but they caught nothing all night.

4 At dawn Jesus was standing on the beach, but the disciples couldn't see who he was. 5 He called out, "Fellows, have you caught any fish?"

"No," they replied.

All of us get stuck in medians sometimes. It's as much a problem for people as it is an issue for mallards. Whenever you and I are stuck, the first and immediate need of the moment is NOT dealing with whatever got us into the median. The first order of business is addressing our fear. Although fear is a secondary emotion (the result of something deeper), it is the very thing that will keep us stuck. It makes sense, doesn't it? Certainly a collision between a duckling and an on-coming mini-van isn't going to go in the duck's favor. So fear becomes in one sense quite helpful, as it can keep a duckling from a needless fatality.

Nevertheless, fear also keeps a duck from moving on into a life of freedom where they can live with significance on the other side of their rescue. You see, ducks are often fearful of the hands that reach out to save because they don't fully understand the intentions of their savior.

~ ~ ~ ~ ~

In John 21 we find Peter stuck in a median of fear. He's betrayed Jesus three times (cf. John 18) and failed to follow through on his own commitment to stay by Jesus' side. So Peter's bailed on Jesus. He's turned coward in an effort to save his own backside. He's left his best friend and Master in the lurch and, after Jesus' crucifixion and death, stands in a self-made median of fear.

The situation Peter finds himself in comes out of his own conscious choice. I say this because Jesus had already conveyed his intentions by offering him a place of peace. If you look at John 20:19–20, you'll note that Jesus appeared to the disciples (including Peter) and said, "Peace be with you." But Peter hadn't received Jesus' offer of peace. He didn't believe Jesus could ever forgive his failings, and so he decided to head for the median of fear.

~ ~ ~ ~ ~

Decisions like Peter's are typically backward in nature. Notice in our biblical text how Peter went back to his trade as a fisherman. He did so because he believed it would be a safe place to retreat. It was his former life, and he knew the ins and outs of it better than most. So it appeared like a comfortable safety net. In actuality though, the safety of fishing was really a guise for fear. It was an excuse to avoid what needed dealing with.

What did Peter need to face? Well, Peter needed to face the one he had hurt. Peter needed to face Jesus and deal with this broken relationship, but the thought of it terrified him. Have you ever gone back to something safe? Have you ever, out of fear, chosen the route of pursuing what you once knew so well? Have you ever used the past to keep from having to deal with the present … with what needs dealing with? Peter's decision to go back to fishing is relational avoidance, and as such it becomes a convenient and easy distraction from the fear of facing Jesus.

~ ~ ~ ~ ~

I once met with a guy who had contacted me because he needed to pray with a pastor. He had been attending church for only a short while, and so

I was glad he felt like he could reach out for help. Although I didn't know his situation, I prayed ahead of time that God would meet with us and give us the wisdom to tackle whatever the presenting issue(s) might be.

My first impression of him was that he was a deeply distracted man. He kept looking at his watch. He kept receiving cell calls and text messages and responding to each and every one of them (there must have been no less than 10 interruptions in our 50 minutes together). By the end of our time I felt on edge and sensed that nothing I shared had even registered.

The most profound part of meeting with him was learning of his desire to go back to the kind of life he had been living that had caused all of his misery in the first place. He had clearly lost all of his monetary wealth on risky ventures, and yet he was convinced that pursuing more shady business deals would enable him to get rich overnight. I knew that going back to what he had succeeded in beforehand would change nothing and would only continue the rollercoaster of success and loss he had been riding on for years. As I tried to convince him of taking a different path out of his current malaise, he would look at me as though none of my words made sense or were even worthy of consideration. I was surprised at his reaction because the path he had chosen only resulted in lack of sleep, constant worry, loss of family and overall personal distress. I concluded that he was more comfortable with the distraction of past monetary gain and the hopes of making it rich again. When he left my office, I couldn't help but feel sorry for him. He was going to stay perched on his median of fear—fear of letting go of his past and trusting in Jesus for his future.

~ ~ ~ ~

Peter also chooses fear. He chooses his tackle box rather than trusting in the peace Jesus had offered him. Further, Peter's decision not only affects himself but the people around him. Peter says to his brood, "I'm going fishing." His friends—Thomas, Nathanael, the sons of Zebedee and two other disciples—all quack in unison, "We'll come too."

Climbing aboard their floating median of fear, John records how they went out in the boat to fish but throughout the entire evening they caught a whopping nothing! Here's the lesson: medians of fear produce nothing. Did you get that? **When we choose what's safe in order to avoid dealing with what's difficult, we get stuck in fearful immobility.** The outflow is we are rendered completely useless, especially in the areas of life we once prided ourselves in. Fear strips us until we are utterly weak!

Now hold onto your little webbed feet! Before you and I go quacking and flopping into the paved roadside, giving up all hope, we need to get a hold of a profound principle. Jesus speaks to our fear and weakness and says, "My grace is all you need. My power works best in weakness" (2 Corinthians 12:9, NLT). As hard as it may be to accept, the most effective posture you and I can be in is on our backs, helplessly flailing our webbed feet. Take a moment to let this image sink in. Fluffy little you and me, on our backs with feet in the air, close to oncoming traffic.

Why is this posture most effective for you and me? Because a rescue can only be a rescue—and a savior can only be a savior—when the one being rescued and saved cannot rescue or save herself.

So there's Peter ... on his back. There's Peter ... quacking and squawking at his empty fishing nets. There's Peter ... completely helpless and afraid. And to him and the others comes a Savior. He sees Peter. He takes notice of him. He calls out to him. He scoops Peter up into his nail-pierced hand and begins the process of rescue.

ON THE OTHER SIDE OF DAY 1:

Parable Principle: When we choose what's safe in order to avoid dealing with what's difficult, we get stuck in fearful immobility.

Scripture Memory Verse for the Week: *"My grace is all you need. My power works best in weakness" (2 Corinthians 12:9, NLT).*

Questions for Reflection:

1. In what way are you stuck on a median of fear? What would it look like to be rescued there—in your weakness—by Jesus?

2. When you think of weakness and rescue, what experience comes to mind? Jot down some key words, thoughts, insights surrounding that experience.

3. How have you tried to go back to what's comfortable rather than address your fears?

4. If you could be utterly candid with Jesus about some areas of your relationship with him that need dealing with, what fears would you express to him?

Taking a Quack at It:

Take some time to read through John chapter 21 again. Go slowly. Close your eyes. Try to imagine the happenings of this account. Picture the scene. Listen to what is being said. See what is being done. As you do so, ask Jesus to reveal where you might be in this account.

Day 2: "Out of the Median of Independence"

> 6 Then he said, "Throw out your net on the right-hand side of the boat, and you'll get some!" So they did, and they couldn't haul in the net because there were so many fish in it.
>
> 7 Then the disciple Jesus loved said to Peter, "It's the Lord!" When Simon Peter heard that it was the Lord, he put on his tunic (for he had stripped for work), jumped into the water, and headed to shore. 8 The others stayed with the boat and pulled the loaded net to the shore, for they were only about a hundred yards from shore. 9 When they got there, they found breakfast waiting for them—fish cooking over a charcoal fire, and some bread.

Independence can kill. When you're a helpless duck stuck out on a median and scrunched between passing cars, you're headed for a lot of hurt and pain. What's ironic is that the ducklings we found tried to remain completely independent. They ran away from us and our offers of help. Depending on us to rescue them didn't come naturally, and yet, without us, those little ducklings would have gotten flattened on the road.

~ ~ ~ ~ ~

I see this same dynamic all the time in ministry. I'll give you just one example out of countless others. There was once a young woman I met who had been living in a state of independence for a number of years.

She didn't want to get close to anyone, and her fear of depending on others made complete sense. Her parents had rejected her and made it very clear she would always be the black sheep of the family. Her church had only made matters worse. They too had sent her packing, wanting nothing to do with her. So in many ways she had been forced into a life of independence. Yet she had also come to choose it. A life of complete independence was more comfortable than depending on others and running the risk of possibly getting hurt all over again. I mean, really, who wants to go through that kind of experience more than once?

The rejections had initially come her way due to a poor choice she had made years before I met her. She had driven a vehicle while intoxicated. The result was a horrific series of personal injuries she had to overcome and endless lawsuits lodged by the injured party she had collided with. She relived personal regret each and every day, and couldn't bring herself to forgive her past mistake. Her family and church had also been unable to forgive her. So she closed herself off. She locked herself away and lived in deep isolation, completely independent of anyone else. She vowed to never run the risk of being hurt again.

One afternoon I paid her a house call with the help and presence of a female parishioner at my church. The first thing we noticed when we visited her was the darkened interior of her home. Her isolation was palpable with all the shadows and dimly lit lamps that failed to bring life-giving light into the house. The second thing we noticed was the silence. It wasn't a pious setting... it was the silence of loneliness. The third thing I took note of was the use of past tense words. Everything for this woman was in the past. Everything that mattered or brought a smile to her face was pre-collision, before the accident, back then. It struck me in those initial moments that her independence was slowly killing her.

Over the course of several weeks we got to know her. We eventually invited her to come to worship. She had a laundry list of reasons why she couldn't attend, including the most pressing reality—her wheelchair-bound body and lack of a car. We had an answer for every one of her excuses and simply created a rotation of drivers who would pick her up each week, bring her to church and take her back home again. When she realized it was useless to stay on the defensive and that we were interested in her as a broken, isolated, full-of-regrets person, she cried in disbelief. She ended up coming to church and, over time, her smiling presence became valued by many people in the church. We loved having her in our community. As she allowed herself to become dependent on us, she began to heal and draw close to Jesus

~ ~ ~ ~ ~

Take a close look at the biblical text for the day. Peter has moved into a life of independence. Out of his broken past (denying Jesus three times) he's gone back to fishing and went so far as to announce his intentions with no desire that anyone join him (cf. John 21:3). The result of his decision is nothing less than a bunch of empty nets. If he keeps this up, he'll die of starvation. Jesus knows this, and the first thing he does is call out to Peter (and the others) and ask how they're faring in their independence. It's not a cruel question, this reminder that they've caught nothing all night; it's simply emphasizing the state of things apart from his saving power. It's the way Jesus shows Peter that he can never really go back to what he once was and succeed at it. It's the empty nets of Peter's own effort that begin to break down his move toward independence and remind him (and the others) of their need for Jesus.

~ ~ ~ ~ ~

Invitations to draw near to love and healing are what Jesus does best. He invites Peter to take the empty nets and throw them off the starboard side of the boat. Jesus confidently asserts the result will be a gargantuan catch. Now let's think on this for a moment. The physical movement of the net is miniscule. We're talking several feet; perhaps less than nine. So is there really a school of fish ready for the taking a few feet away from where Peter and the others had been fishing throughout the night-time hours? Or is this less about the physical movement of the nets and more about becoming dependent on the voice that calls through the fog and into their desperate situation?

Peter could have ignored the voice of Jesus. I mean really, this guy knows more about how to catch water-dwelling prizes than anyone. But he doesn't ignore it. Peter doesn't flop off the median and run the other way in an effort to maintain his independence; rather, Peter responds to the voice with humble obedience. This act of obedience brings him back to depending on Jesus, and the result is life-giving. The nets are full of living and moving fish. This miracle of the countless fish that got swallowed into the nets is a lesson that life is never intended to be lived at a distance from others. The Lord's desire is for us to completely depend on him through obedience and humility. The nets are bulging and about to capsize the boat. Peter hears from the disciple "Jesus loved" that it's no stranger calling out to them, but the Lord Himself! Peter cannonballs off of the railings of the vessel and freestyles it all the way to shore. Dripping wet and out of breath, Peter steps out of his independence and waits by the water's edge. Jesus is there and Peter's astounded to realize that during the breaking of the dawn Jesus has already baited, set the hooks, and reeled in enough scaly behemoths to feed all of the hungry men. Peter is speechless. As he walks into the glow of the campfire, Peter signals his willingness to depend on Jesus.

ON THE OTHER SIDE OF DAY 2:

Parable Principle: Independence can kill.

Scripture Memory Verse for the Week: *"My grace is all you need. My power works best in weakness"* (2 Corinthians 12:9, NLT).

Questions for Reflection:

1. What's the most recent experience you've had of being rejected by people you love?

2. Do you consider yourself to be an independent person? If so, why do you value being self-reliant?

3. Are there areas in your life where you can't make it alone? If so, what are they?

4. What would it look like if you depended on Jesus?

5. How would life change if you began to depend on others?

6. Call to mind a time when you freestyled it back to Jesus as fast as you could. (If you never have, what would it look like if you did today?) What drew you back to Jesus?

7. One of the realities of drawing close to Jesus is experiencing his nourishment. In our text it's baked bread and grilled fish... its friendship over a fire of shared food. What kind of nourishment is Jesus longing to give you? Are you willing to take it in? Why or why not?

Taking a Quack at It:

Commit this breath-prayer to memory and say it often throughout the course of the day: "Lord Jesus Christ, Son of the living God, have mercy on me, a sinner."

DAY 3: "OUT OF THE MEDIAN OF SHAME"

> 10 "Bring some of the fish you've just caught," Jesus said. 11 So Simon Peter went aboard and dragged the net to the shore. There were 153 large fish, and yet the net hadn't torn.
>
> 12 "Now come and have some breakfast!" Jesus said. None of the disciples dared to ask him, "Who are you?" They knew it was the Lord. 13 Then Jesus served them the bread and the fish. 14 This was the third time Jesus had appeared to his disciples since he had been raised from the dead.

"You ought to be ashamed of yourself!" I never once thought of this phrase when I approached mama duck. I didn't scold her. I didn't berate her. I didn't chase her into freedom with the force of justified shame. I didn't begrudge her. I didn't remind her of what she should have done and didn't. Nope. I simply felt compassion.

Compassion means being conscious of another's pain with a desire to ease it. Compassion lessens the shame that might come out of bad decisions. Where shame can cause a person to hang his/her head, compassion encourages and builds up. It raises the head of the recipient.

Peter has reason to hang his head. Peter messed up. Peter "shouldn't have" and he went ahead and did. Peter is worthy of incrimination. In our context we'd say that Peter is facing a rather hefty lawsuit; further, we'd egg Jesus on. We'd encourage Jesus to lay Peter flat, to give him a good raking over; to say, in no uncertain terms, that Peter "ought to be ashamed of himself!"

~ ~ ~ ~

Now take a deep breath. Grab a hold of your molting feathers! Jesus not only doesn't shame Peter, he invites Peter to take pride in something he couldn't have accomplished without Jesus' help. Jesus says, "Bring some of the fish you've just caught." Huh? Ummm... excuse me, Jesus, Peter didn't catch anything all night long! In fact, Peter's whole purpose for fishing had been to avoid Jesus and the pain of his own failings. Nevertheless, Jesus gives Peter the gift of compassion. He knows Peter's shame. He understands Peter has no area in life he can take pride in anymore. So Jesus gives Peter reason to feel better about himself: "the fish you've caught."

Peter looks at the bulging nets of fish. This catch is worthy of the record books, and Jesus has given him reason to see in the prize-winning catch his name, his calloused hands, his own sense of self-worth and esteem. Peter raises his head because he knows the invitation has less to do with fish and more to do with being released from shame. Peter is no longer on the defensive, trying to dodge Jesus' disappointment and anger. Peter understands that Jesus has his best interest in mind and wants to get on with alleviating the burden Peter's been carrying ever since the rooster crowed. Peter's heart begins to open to Jesus. The Lord knows it, and the work of healing can begin.

~ ~ ~ ~ ~

He was a hulking sixteen-year-old at 6-foot-5 and 350 pounds. Although I've got some height, I always found myself feeling microscopic around him. His presence was intimidating. Yet apart from his size, he was lacking in every other area of his life. He was inadequate at school and several years behind his peers. His home life was filled with conflict, and when I say conflict I'm talking about knifings, shootings, drugs and misery. Further, he was lacking financially. His family had no money. Most profound of all, he was poor relationally. He was estranged from his dad and had to watch his mom literally give herself away to other men to help bring income into the home. This young man lived in shame. Shame could have had the final say in his life. It didn't. Through the ministry of the church, this sixteen-year-old began to raise his head little by little. I could see the self-revulsion fade from his eyes every time I spotted him. I watched as the new-found love and acceptance—hope really—began to bring personal worth into his life. Jesus was at work.

When Jesus is at work in the life of a broken individual, it can be uncomfortable for the people who are watching the healing process take place. Think of Peter. He's larger than life and master of the seas! Yet he's shame-faced, able to catch nothing, filled with personal regrets, and living in a place of relational estrangement from Jesus. Jesus calls out. Peter strips down to his skivvies and swims back to shore. I wonder what Peter's companions must have thought when they looked on. Were they anxious, dumbfounded and embarrassed? Did they assume Jesus would give Peter a good scolding? Regardless, Peter knows it's Jesus, and his only desire is to get to him because he needs Jesus to do something that no one else can. He needs Jesus to take away his shame and offer relational acceptance. So Jesus gives him ownership of the catch and an invite to a brunch on the seashore. Peter's head hangs a little less low as a result.

Our hopeless teenager also needed Jesus to do something for him. He needed ownership over something. He needed to be invited in. He needed to experience acceptance and personal worth. So that's what we gave him. He was invited to run our Power Point slides for our morning worship services, and this invitation was very important to him. You see, although he had a lot of shame in his life, the biggest area of defeat was the fact that he couldn't read. The equation of dyslexia and the layered areas of personal brokenness at home created the sum of impossibility. He couldn't get a handle on becoming literate. But here's the thing, although he couldn't read, he knew his own name. And so there we'd be in the middle of worship, singing out a song with the music playing, and I'd hear his peers lovingly cue him as they whispered his name. They'd call out his name, and he'd hit the spacebar and the slide would change. He felt valuable. He felt invited in and accepted. He was able to be a part of a catch of fish he had no part in landing. I can remember feeling a little uneasy. Often the slides lagged behind the song or the sermon. Yet whenever I looked in his eyes and sensed his self-worth on the rise, I knew the most important thing was that hulking kid, who had never been entrusted with a single thing, coming out of shame.

That's what Jesus felt when he saw Peter. He saw a man who had broken a deep bond of trust. Certainly Jesus never needed to entrust him with a single thing, yet he called to him: "'Bring some of the fish you've just caught.' So Simon Peter went aboard and dragged the net to the shore. There were 153 large fish, and yet the net hadn't torn" (John 21:11, NLT).

What comes next is unbelievable. Think for a moment. Jesus was betrayed by Peter. Jesus was abandoned by all of his disciples the night of his arrest. He had every reason to sit in solitude and share none of the fish or bread. If he had wanted to, he could have made sure their nets stayed empty. They could have been brought to his side shame-faced and hungry. But Jesus takes a completely different approach. Jesus doesn't shame, he serves. "Then Jesus served them the bread and the fish. This was the third time Jesus had appeared to his disciples since he had been raised from the dead" (John 21:13–14, NLT).

Jesus serves intentionally. Jesus serves bread and fish during his third appearance to his disciples. He does so because he knows that "3" is a pretty significant number to Peter. It's the number of the inner circle he used to be a part of with James and John. It's also the number of times Peter betrayed Jesus. So in this third appearance Jesus taps into the highest point of Peter's experiences with him and the lowest. They culminate and come together in this first breakfast after the Last Supper—in this third resurrection appearance.

I've often heard that things come in threes. Whenever there's a funeral, some sheepish parishioner will say to me, "You know what they say pastor, things come in threes." I've also heard the same when it comes to weddings or people in need of assistance. We tend to group things in threes. Maybe this notion first started with Peter. If he coined the phrase I wouldn't be surprised. But Peter learned in this experience that **when it comes to life on the other side of one's rescue, grace—not shame—is the final word.**

~ ~ ~ ~ ~

To come out of the median of shame is far from easy. Yet Jesus is able to lift our heads if we let him. He has our best interests in mind if we'll only trust him and respond with faith. Jesus wants to serve us. This is an invitation to nourishment we had no part in creating and really don't deserve. He offers it freely to us; and all of our best and worst experiences culminate in this time with Jesus, where we learn that his desire to move us on into freedom begins with ridding us of shame.

ON THE OTHER SIDE OF DAY 3:

Parable Principle: When it comes to life on the other side of one's rescue, grace—not shame—is the final word.

Scripture Memory Verse for the Week: *"My grace is all you need. My power works best in weakness"* (2 Corinthians 12:9, NLT).

Questions for Reflection:

1. Has there been a time in your life when you've been told that you "ought to be ashamed of yourself"? What surrounded that experience?
2. Is there good and bad shame? If so, what are the differences between the two?
3. Has Jesus ever entered your life and alleviated your shame? How did he work in your life to take it away?
4. In what ways has Jesus served you even when you've hurt or betrayed him?
5. How can you serve others like Jesus has served you?
6. How do appropriate relational boundaries impact what it looks like to serve others (especially those who've been hurtful to you)?

Taking a Quack at It:

List the ways God has exhibited grace to you in your life. Now stare at the list for a good five minutes. Take in who God is and has been in the context of who you are and have been.

DAY 4: "OUT OF THE MEDIAN OF INDIFFERENCE"

> *15 After breakfast Jesus asked Simon Peter, "Simon son of John, do you love me more than these?"*
>
> *"Yes, Lord," Peter replied, "you know I love you."*
>
> *"Then feed my lambs," Jesus told him.*
>
> *16 Jesus repeated the question: "Simon son of John, do you love me?"*
>
> *"Yes, Lord," Peter said, "you know I love you."*
>
> *"Then take care of my sheep," Jesus said.*

Rescued into a Life of Gratitude

17 A third time he asked him, "Simon son of John, do you love me?"

Peter was hurt that Jesus asked the question a third time. He said, "Lord, you know everything. You know that I love you."

Jesus said, "Then feed my sheep.

18 "I tell you the truth, when you were young, you were able to do as you liked; you dressed yourself and went wherever you wanted to go. But when you are old, you will stretch out your hands, and others will dress you and take you where you don't want to go." 19 Jesus said this to let him know by what kind of death he would glorify God. Then Jesus told him, "Follow me."

When I drove past that blur of fluffy yellow, flat on its back, indifference said it was someone else's problem. I could go on with my day, having absolutely no culpability, even if every single last bird had been run over. No Boston policeman would have come looking for me. No Miranda rights would have been spoken. I wouldn't have faced any repercussions in connection with a situation that had gone south. (Sorry, I can't help myself.) Indifference is easy, isn't it? It's the Dollar General of the conscience. Indifference costs hardly anything, and even if there's an ounce of guilt, there's always the surplus of others one can point to and say, "Well, they didn't do anything either!"

If intentionality is what made a way for ducklings in my daughter's storybook, indifference is what keeps a mama duck and her babies on a dangerous median. Intentionality and indifference are relational antonyms. As we continue in our biblical passage, we learn one of the big lessons in living on the other side of our rescue: **We must be willing to move past the place of indifference and into a life of intention.**

~ ~ ~ ~ ~

Jesus, Peter and the others have just finished up breakfast. Crumbs of bread mingle with sand. Baked fish scales and charred bones begin to glow a hot red as they disintegrate on the white coals. An awkward relational pause ensues. What's going to happen with Jesus and Peter?

Just as this question begins to percolate in everyone's mind, Jesus invites Peter to take an early morning walk with him along the seashore. Just imagine how the sound of crunching sand must have entered the scene.

Crunch, crunch, crunch... the noise of the walk filled the air as Peter wondered what might happen next. A mixture of wanting to be there and wanting to be somewhere far, far away from there must have crowded Peter's mind. He's uneasy. If you've ever been reunited with someone you were once close to, but the relationship took a turn because of your indifference, then you know exactly what Peter must have been feeling.

But what about Jesus? What's he feeling? The text implies that Jesus is filled with anticipation. Whereas Peter might assume this is the end of their relationship, Jesus sees this moment as an opportunity for Peter to move closer to his Savior. This time with Peter is an intentional and life-giving moment for Jesus to leverage.

~ ~ ~ ~ ~

I had been indifferent for more than a year. Although Tracey and Chatham (our daughter hadn't been born yet) had gone with me back to Kentucky for a year-long, on-campus portion of my doctoral program at Asbury Theological Seminary, I had done nothing to honor their willingness to change life on the fly. My doctoral thesis was unfinished, and I had no intention of completing it. I was too busy to fuss with it. Yet my indifference caused pain in Tracey. I knew it and had avoided the conversation for a long time.

One afternoon we decided to take a boat across Boston Harbor to the city. We loved to spend time on Long Warf, especially in the growing warmth of the springtime. What I didn't anticipate was a concealed picture that my wife smuggled with her on our day trip venture. After enjoying a scenic boat ride, we arrived at the dock and disembarked near a public park right next to the North End of the city. Tracey seized the moment.

"Tim, before we go forward with our day together, I've got to get real with you about something that's bothering me."

Although I had a gut feeling of what was coming, I said, "What's up, hon?"

Tracey pulled out the picture. It was a snapshot of my doctoral peers at their recent graduation. Doctoral certificates were in their hands and big smiles were on their faces.

Tracey looked at me in complete silence. She wanted the image to sink in. I grew defensive. "Great for them," I remarked sarcastically.

Tracey continued in her silence for some time. I looked angrily out at the harbor, not wanting to face my unfinished work.

"But I'm too busy, Trace!" I wasn't budging. More time passed. Finally Tracey spoke.

"I know you're busy and that the church isn't easy to lead, but this indifference is really getting to me. You've got to finish your dissertation if for no other reason than to honor me and our son. We moved our lives back to Kentucky for you. Now don't get me wrong, it was a great year and all, but we sacrificed for you. You need to seriously get off of your butt and get going on this." She handed me the picture as a reminder of where I was and where I could get to with some intention.

I knew she was serious. I knew she was right too. My indifference had been called out by my wife, and from that moment on, I set to work with the goal of honoring the season of life they had given me.

~ ~ ~ ~ ~

This is the final conversation Jesus is going to have with Peter. He's already offered him peace. He has one more objective.

> "Simon son of John, do you love me more than these?"
>
> "Yes, Lord," Peter replied, "you know I love you."
>
> "Then feed my lambs," Jesus told him.
>
> Jesus repeated the question: "Simon son of John, do you love me?"
>
> "Yes, Lord," Peter said, "you know I love you."
>
> "Then take care of my sheep," Jesus said.
>
> A third time he asked him, "Simon son of John, do you love me?"
>
> Peter was hurt that Jesus asked the question a third time. He said, "Lord, you know everything. You know that I love you."
>
> Jesus said, "Then feed my sheep" (John 21:15–17, NLT).

Jesus is candid. Peter is wary. Jesus is painfully forthright. Peter is cut to the heart. Yet, through the encounter, what could have continued unchecked—namely, indifference—is called out, and Peter is left with one option: become intentional and honor Jesus... or... continue down the path of indifference and dishonor the one who's sacrificed everything.

Now there's a lot to this interchange between Jesus and Peter. There's the literal Greek rendering for "love" and how it morphs and changes throughout the conversation. There are the three questions many believe match Peter's three denials and the significance of each. There's also the intentional wording Jesus uses that seems to bring to light previous presumptuous statements Peter had made that his love for Jesus excelled that of his peers. I'd encourage you to pursue these insights, but what I want to hone in on is the dynamic of living intentionally versus living indifferently.

The core question Jesus asks ("Do you love me?") is a question of intention. Love (if it's authentic) is never indifferent. To love someone means in every moment, in every conversation, in every action there is bound up in that love great intention. Love does not allow indifference. Hatred does. Slothfulness is a byproduct of indifference. Selfishness can certainly lead to indifference... but love... love and indifference cannot coexist. The Apostle Paul says, "Don't just pretend to love others. Really love them. Hate what is wrong. Hold tightly to what is good. Love each other with genuine affection, and take delight in honoring each other" (Romans 12:9–10, NLT). This is the kind of life Jesus is calling Peter into.

Jesus' desire is to rescue Peter. This rescue out of the median of indifference is not a rescue for a momentary segment of time or a past date that Peter might celebrate every once in a while as he turns around and goes back to life as it's always been. Sometimes we assume that when Jesus rescues us the purpose is getting us across the street safely and shooing us into the woods. That's it. That's the extent. Yet we fail to open ourselves to the truth that Jesus rescues us into an intentional life. Jesus rescues us, for a purpose that has far-reaching consequences in how we live on the other side of that rescue throughout the remainder of whatever days God gifts us.

"Do you love me?"

"Then feed my lambs."

"Do you love me?"

"Take care of my sheep."

"Do you love me?"

"Then feed my sheep."

What Jesus is getting at is precisely what Peter missed entirely the evening he denied his Lord. Jesus is saying to Peter that if he's going to be rescued, he must come to terms with living a life that does away with indifference. He can't deny again. He can't go forward in the Kingdom of Heaven and save his own skin if things should get difficult and scary. Peter's got to take in the Lord's expectation of intention. This explains why later in the conversation Jesus says, "'I tell you the truth, when you were young, you were able to do as you liked; you dressed yourself and went wherever you wanted to go. But when you are old, you will stretch out your hands, and others will dress you and take you where you don't want to go.' Jesus said this to let him know by what kind of death he would glorify God. Then Jesus told him, 'Follow me'" (John 21:18–19, NLT). What Jesus is saying is that the days of Peter making choices that keep him comfortable and indifferent have come to an end. The next time Peter feels compelled to turn tail and run, he won't. Instead, he'll willingly stretch out his hands and allow others to dress him and take him where he doesn't want to go… namely, to his suffering and death for the sake of Jesus.

If this is Jesus' call on the life of Peter…

If this is Jesus' image of what life is like in the Kingdom of Heaven…

If this is what we can expect to be his desire for you and me on the other side of our rescue…

What will it look like in our lives if we respond to and live out this life of intention?

ON THE OTHER SIDE OF DAY 4:

Parable Principle: We must be willing to move past the place of indifference and into a life of intention.

Scripture Memory Verse for the Week: *"My grace is all you need. My power works best in weakness" (2 Corinthians 12:9, NLT).*

Questions for Reflection:

1. How do you define "indifference" from what you've experienced and witnessed in your own life?

2. Do you agree that intentionality and indifference are relational antonyms? Why or why not?

3. Indifference is the Dollar General of the conscience because it's so cheap to live off of. How have you chosen indifference in your life? Why?

4. To be a follower of Jesus means we are to become intentional in the way we love. How would becoming intentional change your life?

Taking a Quack at It:

In this present moment there may be an area of your life where indifference is comfortable for you. Why have you become indifferent? Prayerfully ask the Lord to help you become intentional today. As you pray, try to imagine what intentionality might look like in that area of your life you've named.

DAY 5: "OUT OF THE MEDIAN OF ATTRACTION"

> *20 Peter turned around and saw behind them the disciple Jesus loved—the one who had leaned over to Jesus during supper and asked, "Lord, who will betray you?" 21 Peter asked Jesus, "What about him, Lord?"*
>
> *22 Jesus replied, "If I want him to remain alive until I return, what is that to you? As for you, follow me." 23 So the rumor spread among the community of believers that this disciple wouldn't die. But that isn't what Jesus said at all. He only said, "If I want him to remain alive until I return, what is that to you?"*

You're probably familiar with the term, "herd mentality," or, "going with the herd." For our purposes I'll change it a little to "flock mentality," or, "going with the flock." In my experience on the median I learned quite quickly that what mama duck, sister duck or brother duck does is what all the others do. If there's panic in one duckling, ALL of the ducks begin to panic. If one duckling flops off the median and onto the road, ALL the ducks begin flopping off the median and onto the road. Perhaps a close cousin to this is the old saying, "What's good for the goose is good for the gander."

A flock mentality can easily permeate our life in Jesus. We tend to want to get our little bills in the lives of the ducks we know or are in relationship with. We want to glean the latest gossip on how someone else is doing in their life with Jesus. We want to know how that other duckling gives at church. We want to understand the commitment that other mallard we know has to God's Word, or their small group, or their involvement in the duckling ministry. We want to know not just to know, but to have the ability to do the same (or less).

Jesus' disciples had always been jostling with each other and comparing their devotion to Jesus. There is a sense in the four Gospels that Jesus had to speak to their competitive natures on more than one occasion, reminding them that greatness in the Kingdom has to do with being last and serving the others. Yet the ways of the Kingdom are difficult to get a handle on. We find ourselves easily distracted.

~ ~ ~ ~ ~

Although he was getting on in years, he still acted like a child. He saw the devotion of the young people. He heard their commitments to the good news of Jesus. He witnessed their sacrifices to be a part of the local church and to allow the love of Jesus to break into their hip-hop culture. But what he took note of, he didn't like. He made his convictions quite clear... in private that is.

"You know, pastor, the founding pastor of this church never meant to reach those people."

It was a moment in time I didn't quite know what to do with. I wondered if I really heard what had just been spoken. *Surely he's not referring to their economic status. Certainly he can't be referring to the color of their skin.*

Shortly after his remark to me, I wasn't at all surprised to find a letter in my mailbox. "Pastor, this was our last Sunday in worship. We've decided to attend another congregation. We wish you all the best."
I couldn't help but pity the man. He left because he couldn't help but be distracted by the devotion of the young people. Jesus had entered their lives and was transforming them in the context of their culture and the way they spoke, sang, understood things and communicated things. He was looking at them (rather than Jesus), and he couldn't take his eyes off of what he was seeing. Jesus was making a way even for them!

~ ~ ~ ~

Peter also suffers from a distracted gaze. Even after his one-on-one time with Jesus, Peter can't help but notice a fellow duckling, "the disciple Jesus loved." John recounts, "Peter turned around and saw behind them the disciple Jesus loved—the one who had leaned over to Jesus during supper and asked, 'Lord, who will betray you?' Peter asked Jesus, 'What about him, Lord'" (John 21:20–21).

What about him? What about her, Lord? We often ask these kinds of questions because it's easier to focus on another person's life in Christ rather than on our own. What Peter's up to here in the text is a process of gauging the life Jesus is calling him to versus what Jesus might be calling others to. Peter has just learned he'll most likely suffer a great deal on account of Jesus. So Peter's chewing on what's facing him and the natural course of thought is to begin to wonder if John… or Thomas… or Nathanael… or the sons of Zebedee… are going to face a similar fate. There's a sense of comfort in shared misery. Further, if others have only painless futures awaiting them, then perhaps I can bring the point to bear on Jesus and he'll reconsider my fate.

Entertaining a distracted gaze is always an "out" when it comes to the life of faith. It's the way we decide whether we've really got to accept what Jesus has for us or if we can get into the safe and comfortable company of the flock we're in and follow their flight pattern into a less severe reality. Jesus has nothing to do with it. He doesn't buy it. He doesn't allow it. He doesn't even give a moment of time to it. "If I want him to remain alive until I return, what is that to you? As for you, follow me" (John 21:22).

Our feathers get a little ruffled with Jesus' reply. He's not going to enable my flock mentality and the traction it gives me to refrain from follow-

Rescued into a Life of Gratitude

ing... from suffering... from having difficulties on account of my life in him. But Jesus doesn't care about our ruffled feathers. Jesus' only concern is that we gaze on him and follow him. It takes intentional effort to turn our eyes upon Jesus, but it's the only way we can avoid staying on the median with the flock.

The hymn "Turn Your Eyes upon Jesus"[2] is simple in the words of its chorus, but powerful in its truth. "Turn your eyes upon Jesus, look full in his wonderful face, and the things of earth will grow strangely dim in the light of his glory and grace." As we turn our eyes upon Jesus, it does become strange how the concerns of the flock begin to fade. We see less of ourselves, less of those we tend to pay attention to, and more and more of Jesus. This shift of focus helps us to follow him regardless of what others choose. It brings an end to competition. It keeps us from worrying about the other person. Contented, we follow Jesus even if it means something quite different for us. As we follow, we soon become more attracted to Jesus and less so with the opinions and directions of others.

ON THE OTHER SIDE OF DAY 5:

Parable Principle: Entertaining a distracted gaze is always an "out" when it comes to the life of faith.

Scripture Memory Verse for the Week: *"My grace is all you need. My power works best in weakness" (2 Corinthians 12:9, NLT).*

Questions for Reflection:

1. Do you suffer from a distracted gaze? If so, name the person(s) and ponder why you choose to keep your eye on him/her.

2. Do you agree that we tend to gauge our life in Jesus by what others are experiencing? If so, how has this hindered you?

3. What are some seasons in life when you have had the ability to focus on Jesus? What enabled you to be focused on him?

4. Are there areas in your life that you're struggling in right now? If so, how can you keep on following Jesus regardless of whether others have it easier than you?

Taking a Quack at It:

Confession breaks the habit of having a flock mentality or being in competition with one another. Confession unites us as we share our deepest weaknesses and failures with a trusted friend. Perhaps there is someone you can confess your struggle to when it comes to being distracted or concerned with how someone else is (or is not) following Jesus. Maybe you also want to confess your reluctance to live the life Jesus is leading you into. Think through who you want to share with, if the relationship is appropriate to do so in, and what and how you want to share.

DAY 6: "INTO A LIFE OF GRATITUDE"

It's easy to assume that the life of Jesus is about "outs." People will sometimes say, "Jesus saved me out of addiction." "Jesus brought me out of shame." "Jesus took me out of personal brokenness." I don't mean to diminish the value of these kinds of experiences for those who have them; certainly freedom from sin and bondage is at the heart of our life in Jesus. Nevertheless, it is also important to understand that the life of Jesus is about "ins." Jesus saves us into a life that is lived on the other side of our rescue.

If you're wondering about this point, just think for a moment about the Hebrews who were brought out of Egypt in the exodus. We marvel at the wonder-working power of God. Yet if we compare the amount of biblical literature devoted to the exodus versus the amount of writing pertaining to what it means to be the people of God on the other side of their rescue, we have to conclude that the weight of attention is with the latter rather than the former. God is ultimately concerned with the kind of life we lead once we're freed.

~ ~ ~ ~ ~

If I were to capture my hope for the ducklings we rescued and their new-found life, it would entail the word gratitude. I would want those ducklings and their mama to be grateful. I don't have a basis for this focus other than being honest with you and understanding that I could hope for another 101 things. Yet it's gratitude that I land on because I believe it's the natural desire for the one doing the rescuing to hope that the recipients understand the scope of what's been accomplished on their behalf.

This point makes me think of one of my favorite films, *Saving Private Ryan*[3]. This movie is in many ways an adult version of *Make Way for Ducklings*. It's a WWII story about Captain Miller and his Charlie Company, whose sole purpose is to make a way for Private Ryan to get back home so that his mom doesn't have to grieve the loss of yet another son (she's already lost three others within just days of each other). During the course of trying to find Ryan—and then, upon finding him, setting him on a course to freedom—Captain Miller and his company come under heavy fire in Ramelle, France. Miller is mortally wounded. As he lies dying, with Private Ryan looking on, he says to Ryan, "Earn this. Earn it."

I cried as I watched this ending scene in the movie because I know what Miller's saying. He's saying to Ryan that he'd better live a grateful life on the other side of all of the sacrifice done on his behalf. In other words, their rescue of him had better mean something more than a trite sentimentalism. It'd better have impact.

~ ~ ~ ~ ~

Jesus has rescued us. If we had witnessed his suffering and death on the cross, we'd want to shield our eyes and stop our ears. We'd have a difficult time stomaching the gruesome nature of Jesus' sacrifice. It'd be a recurring nightmare throughout the rest of our days. That painful. That dreadful. That much offered up for you and for me.

Peter witnessed Jesus' suffering firsthand. He heard it. He saw it. He reacted to it in a selfish way. Yet Jesus rescued Peter. Jesus reached out to him through his own suffering and death and invited him into a new life. A life of significance. A life of gratitude.

Just like Peter, Jesus is asking you and me what we are doing with what he's done. Is it meaningless? Has it spiraled into fake sentimentalism? Does it have no impact or meaning? Is it simply, "I'm good to go when it comes to heaven. Now let's get back to living it up like hell"?

One of the primary ways we can begin to live on the other side of our rescue is to become grateful. Gratitude is at the core when it comes to living for Jesus because it is our natural response to all that the Lord has done for us. Gratitude is the reason we belt out songs in worship. It's why we give thanks at the Lord's Supper. It's the "why" behind why we pray at all. Gratitude is how we process our rescue on a daily basis.

The Apostle Paul says, "Be thankful in all circumstances, for this is God's will for you who belong to Christ Jesus" (I Thessalonians 5:18). Get that? God's will! God's will is essentially simple. God's will is that we are thankful… i.e., grateful! Why? Because all of eternity backs our rescue—and all of eternity is a result of our rescue. We get to live freely in the rescuing love of Jesus throughout all of eternity because he has done something for us we couldn't do. He's rescued us. He's scooped us up and carried us across what would have killed us. He's set us down into freedom and doesn't shoo us on; rather, he walks and often leads us into a life of gratitude. With every bend and turn, every joy and sorrow, we get to experience what he longs to afford us: compassionate, tender, servant-like love to live a new life. A life of freedom.

ON THE OTHER SIDE OF DAY 6:

Parable Principle: One of the primary ways we can begin to live on the other side of our rescue is to become grateful.

Scripture Memory Verse for the Week: *"My grace is all you need. My power works best in weakness" (2 Corinthians 12:9, NLT).*

Questions for Reflection:

1. Have you tended to view life with Jesus as an experience of coming "out" of brokenness? If so, how would it change things to understand the invitational nature of what it means to follow him?

2. Do you agree that God's core desire for you is to experience gratitude?

3. Are you a grateful person? If so, why? If not, why not?

4. Would you agree that God's will is that we be thankful in all circumstances? If so, what kind of thankfulness is the Apostle Paul talking about?

Taking a Quack at It:

Gratitude can become a reality for you. Each evening for the next week, jot down 3 simple things you're grateful for. It'll only cost you a few minutes. Maybe you're grateful for an ice cream sandwich you enjoyed after lunch. Perhaps it's a good friend you got to talk with or a child you enjoyed sharing time with. Whatever the reason for gratitude, name it and give God thanks. Over a few short days you'll begin to experience a new way of seeing and experiencing daily life.

DAY 7: REST

Worship in community.

Enjoy the presence of loved ones.

Take time to take note of God's creation.

Reflect on this past week.

Commit this coming week to the Lord.

ENDNOTES

1. Robert McCloskey, *Make Way for Ducklings*. New York, NY: Penguin Putnam Books for Young Readers, 1999.

2. Helen H. Lemmel, *The United Methodist Hymnal*. Nashville, TN: The United Methodist Publishing House, 1989, #349.

3. Robert Rodat (writer), Steven Spielberg (director), *Saving Private Ryan*, Paramount Pictures, 1998.

PARABLE 2

Wheat-Cracker and Jelly-Bean Sandwiches: Rescued into a Life of Obedience

Every parent wonders from time to time if it was worth it. Looking back, I can say beyond a shadow of a doubt it was worth it, even if my belly still rumbles in disagreement. You see, wheat crackers and jelly beans can wreak havoc on your stomach, but the memory of making the cutest girl in the world smile overshadows the uneasy reaction to having to develop a whole new palate. Let me explain.

I am my daughter's fictitious horse. Even though I don't have a name other than "horsey," you'd think my daughter had owned me for years and years the way she calls out to me and takes care of me. Although I look like a saddle-backed and graying appaloosa, my daughter is convinced I am a stallion on par with Black Beauty or Man-O-War.

Like most children at play, my daughter has a ritual to our game together. She calls me into her room which has been imaginatively transformed into an English stable and farmhouse, and then asks that I get on all fours. Pulling out her winter scarf, Molly tames me by wrapping it around my neck and tying me to the nearest chair, desk or table where I become immovable and safe enough to be worked with. Once anchored, Molly proceeds to draw hooves on my hands and comb my mane (a modest shock of thinning hair). After about thirty minutes of being groomed and becoming a more respectable-looking horse, Molly usually saddles me with a small blanket and proceeds to command, "Giddy-up, horsey!" We ride (really saunter) through the house a time or two. The cat looks on with disgust from his perch on top of the refrigerator. Our dog, Lucy, begins to bark, prance and pounce at me thinking, I'm on all fours to play with her. Having to break character, I'll warn the dog not come too near this steely steed. If I'm stern enough, Lucy retreats and watches from a safe distance. Chatham sometimes spies our stroll through the bramble and country roads of our journey and leaps out as an unexpected bandit or knight, calling us to a duel. A parlay might take place and the victor, after much explaining and diplomacy, is always Molly. Our ride through the English countryside and arrival back "home" usually signals the day's reprieve for my sore knees; however, the task of enduring the next phase of horse life has just begun.

Molly has a little pink step-stool next to her bed. The uppermost of its two steps can be opened, revealing a small wooden compartment. Molly likes to keep her sparkly purple slippers in this top-step compartment so Lucy can't get to them and shred them into a million pieces. As her mom and dad, we love the practical uses of the step-stool. Yet the practical nature of it is not what Molly appreciates most. What Molly likes best is the fact that this top step is not only helpful in protecting her slippers, but also makes a really good trough for a horse.

The trough has held numerous items. Water's been poured inside for me to lap (always a messy business). Apples have found their place in the trough, but Molly usually ends up having to hold them so they don't roll around and get away from me. Carrots have been placed inside for me to eat. There's been cheese, lettuce, uncooked cabbage (quite nasty), cookies, taffy, and much, much more. I can usually stomach everything my daughter puts down into the trough, but one afternoon I had a difficult time swallowing what was offered to me: three wheat-cracker and jelly-bean "sandwiches."

The wheat crackers were the grainy kind my wife buys in the organic section of the grocery store and makes all of us eat. The jelly beans were almost a year old. They had been tucked into one of Molly's handbags and found unexpectedly that afternoon—much to Molly's delight. She sandwiched the crackers and jelly beans, certain her horse would relish this delicacy. I wasn't nearly as confident.

The first sandwich was placed into my mouth before I knew what was happening. In horse-like obedience I began to chew. The wheat cracker crunched and snapped. The jelly beans smushed and congealed. The grainy texture began to mix with the sugary sweet. It wasn't a good acquaintance. Chewing and regretting my station in life, I finally was able to swallow the first helping.

Molly offered the second sandwich with a smile. She truly hoped I was enjoying lunch. I smiled back, not wanting to ruin what had been so sweetly given. I ate, but my stomach began to voice its dislike of what was coming down the pipe. I could tell that Molly was pleased. I neighed in a happy tone (not sure how to do this, but I did). Molly was encouraged.

The third and final sandwich was a real challenge. The old jelly beans and the sweet on whole grain just didn't work too well for my taste. But I didn't want to ruin Molly's imaginative playtime. So when Molly pointed at the third installment of my lunch, I simply closed my eyes and pretended to fall into an upright, horse-like nap. No luck. My eyes popped opened as Molly grabbed the sandwich with one hand, opened my jaw with the other and placed the entrée therein. I began to buck and spit. "Now, horsey," she said, "I know, honey… I know… but this is good for you." I tried to whinny and shy away, but Molly was insistent. Holding my lips closed and pinching my nose shut, she made good and sure the food out of the trough went down. I was sick to my stomach.

~ ~ ~ ~ ~

Now I know what you're thinking: "Tim, if the taste of wheat crackers and jelly beans was that unsavory, why didn't you just refuse or simply steer Molly in a different direction?" Good question. All I can say is that I'm a softy. Molly was so excited to find jelly beans and so confident of her concoction of sweet on wheat that I just couldn't look into her soft brown eyes and refuse. I decided to take it in because Molly's worldview mattered more than mine. She was having the time of her life, and I wanted to support it even if the mere memory of the recipe still sends shivers down my back. Plus, at least it was just crackers and jelly beans. I mean really, some adults will eat almost anything for a buck or two. At least what I ate wasn't still alive or carrying the stench of death and decay. And, more than a buck, I got time with my daughter on her terms and in her imagination. The innocent play of a kindergartner is a short-lived reality; I didn't want to shortcut it.

~ ~ ~ ~ ~

As I pondered the experience of eating wheat crackers and jelly beans, I couldn't help but think of its significance in our life with Jesus. In other words, if journeying into my daughter's world means I've got to stomach something foreign to my sense of taste, surely journeying into my Savior's world means the same on a much grander scale. What it means is the focus of this week. Further, it comes after the first week on our rescue because we've been rescued into a life where one of the first things we realize is the life of Jesus is foreign to our sense of taste. It's a kind of like a wheat-cracker and jelly-bean sandwich. But Jesus offers it to us with the joy of knowing it's ultimately for our good as we follow him on the other side of our rescue.

Biblical Text for Week 2: John 14:6–7; 14:15–15:27

[John 14] 6Jesus told him, "I am the way, the truth, and the life. No one can come to the Father except through me.   7 If you had really known me, you would know who my Father is. From now on, you do know him and have seen him!"

15 "If you love me, obey my commandments. 16 And I will ask the Father, and he will give you another Advocate, who will never leave you. 17 He is the Holy Spirit, who leads into all truth. The world cannot receive him, because it isn't looking for him and doesn't recognize him. But you know him, because he lives with you now and later will be in you. 18 No, I will not abandon you as orphans—I will come to you. 19 Soon the world will no longer see me, but you will see me. Since I live, you also will live. 20 When I am raised to life again, you will know that I am in my Father, and you are in me, and I am in you. 21 Those who accept my commandments and obey them are the ones who love me. And because they love me, my Father will love them. And I will love them and reveal myself to each of them."

22 Judas (not Judas Iscariot, but the other disciple with that name) said to him, "Lord, why are you going to reveal yourself only to us and not to the world at large?"

23 Jesus replied, "All who love me will do what I say. My Father will love them, and we will come and make our home with each of them. 24 Anyone who doesn't love me will not obey me. And remember, my words are not my own. What I am telling you is from the Father who sent me. 25 I am telling you these things now while I am still with you. 26 But when the Father sends the Advocate as my representative—that is, the Holy Spirit—he will teach you everything and will remind you of everything I have told you.

27 "I am leaving you with a gift—peace of mind and heart. And the peace I give is a gift the world cannot give. So don't be troubled or afraid. 28 Remember what I told you: I am going away, but I will come back to you again. If you really loved me, you would be happy that I am going to the Father, who is greater than I am. 29 I have told you these things before they happen so that when they do happen, you will believe.

30 "I don't have much more time to talk to you, because the ruler of this world approaches. He has no power over me, 31 but I will do what the Father requires of me, so that the world will know that I love the Father. Come, let's be going.

[John 15] 1 "I am the true grapevine, and my Father is the gardener. 2 He cuts off every branch of mine that doesn't produce fruit, and he prunes the branches that do bear fruit so they will produce even more. 3 You have already been pruned and purified by the message I have given you. 4 Remain in me, and I will remain in you. For a branch cannot produce fruit if it is severed from the vine, and you cannot be fruitful unless you remain in me.

5 "Yes, I am the vine; you are the branches. Those who remain in me, and I in them, will produce much fruit. For apart from me you can do nothing. 6 Anyone who does not remain in me is thrown away like a useless branch and withers. Such branches are gathered into a pile to be burned. 7 But if you remain in me and my words remain in you, you may ask for anything you want, and it will be granted! 8 When you produce much fruit, you are my true disciples. This brings great glory to my Father.

9 "I have loved you even as the Father has loved me. Remain in my love. 10 When you obey my commandments, you remain in my love, just as I obey my Father's commandments and remain in his love. 11 I have told you these things so that you will be filled with my joy. Yes, your joy will overflow! 12 This is my commandment: Love each other in the same way I have loved you. 13 There is no greater love than to lay down one's life for one's friends. 14 You are my friends if you do what I command. 15 I

no longer call you slaves, because a master doesn't confide in his slaves. Now you are my friends, since I have told you everything the Father told me. 16 You didn't choose me. I chose you. I appointed you to go and produce lasting fruit, so that the Father will give you whatever you ask for, using my name. 17 This is my command: Love each other.

18 "If the world hates you, remember that it hated me first. 19 The world would love you as one of its own if you belonged to it, but you are no longer part of the world. I chose you to come out of the world, so it hates you. 20 Do you remember what I told you? 'A slave is not greater than the master.' Since they persecuted me, naturally they will persecute you. And if they had listened to me, they would listen to you. 21 They will do all this to you because of me, for they have rejected the One who sent me. 22 They would not be guilty if I had not come and spoken to them. But now they have no excuse for their sin. 23 Anyone who hates me also hates my Father. 24 If I hadn't done such miraculous signs among them that no one else could do, they would not be guilty. But as it is, they have seen everything I did, yet they still hate me and my Father. 25 This fulfills what is written in their Scriptures: 'They hated me without cause.'

26 "But I will send you the Advocate—the Spirit of truth. He will come to you from the Father and will testify all about me. 27 And you must also testify about me because you have been with me from the beginning of my ministry.

Day 1: "Becoming Tame"

15 "If you love me, obey my commandments."

When Molly calls on me to play the game "horsey," the story unfolds in a very precise way. The first thing that happens is she becomes my owner and I become tame under her teaching and care. Becoming tame is simple for Molly; it means doing what she says when she says it. "Eat your wheat-cracker and jelly-bean sandwich, horsey!" *Munch... munch... munch* is the expected response. "Horsey, I'm going to put a saddle on you, so just stand still." Carrying Molly on my back and traveling through the house is the expected response. So in Molly's world, becoming tame equals being obedient.

This is essentially what Jesus is getting at in our scripture for the day. "If you love me, obey my commandments" (John 14:14, NLT). My daughter would translate this verse as "a good horsey listens and obeys." It's true; tameness in our life with Jesus equals living obediently. Ponder this truth for a moment. Isn't it profound in its simplicity?

~ ~ ~ ~ ~

When we think of loving Jesus on the other side of our rescue, we often assume love means "feelings." *If I feel a certain way, then I must love Jesus.* This course of thought leads to a life with Jesus based on warm fuzzies. "I feel love for Jesus, so we must be close." "I feel like Jesus loves me today, so he must like who I am." Certainly Jesus doesn't discount our feelings, but the way of living for Jesus that is based on feelings is a treacherous path because feelings are fickle. They change all the time.

If our relationship with Jesus is led by our feelings, then guess what? Our relationship with Jesus will be in a constant state of change. It reminds me of the time I worked with horses back in graduate school. I'd get up at 4:30 a.m. and drive out to a beautiful Kentucky horse farm where I'd clean stalls for a good two hours before coming back home and getting ready for a day of classes. I loved the job and the horses—except for one. In the back corner of the barn, there was a grey appaloosa that was unpredictable. She might like you one day and she might despise you the next. I was always really careful around her because she had been known to buck and kick at people. It was the unknown of what I might face on any given day that kept me at a safe distance from the horse. I never got close to that one. I did to all the others, but that one just wasn't safe enough to be around.

My experience with that horse is similar to what feelings do in our life with Jesus. One day we may desire to follow Jesus with love and passion. The next? Well, we might not feel like following him at all. We could even buck or kick at his presence. You see, living life with Jesus on the basis of feelings leads to relational distance rather than closeness. So there's a taming process we have to go through in order to draw close to Jesus.

~ ~ ~ ~ ~

Jesus' taming process comes from the text for the day: "If you love me, obey my commandments" (John 14:15, NLT). **Obedience is what we**

build our life with Jesus on. Obedience is what we are to expect when we follow Jesus on the other side of our rescue. Obedience is the bit and bridle of our life in Jesus that enables us to live close to him and be used by him.

You may be asking—or perhaps you've asked countless times in the past—how can I show the depth of my love to Jesus, the one who's rescued me? Well, Jesus spells it out clearly. "If you love me, obey my commandments" (John 14:15, NLT). It's that simple.

A horse shows love to its owner through obedience. Through obedience a person can safely ride on a horse. Through obedience a person can expect that the horse will not intentionally buck or kick at him or her. Through obedience a loving owner can get close enough to their horse that they can pet it, feed it, care for it. All of this comes through obedience. Obedience and being a tame "good horsey" are one and the same.

Obedience is how we show love to Jesus. Obedience to what? To Jesus' commandments. The accounts of Jesus' ministry in the gospels are full of teachings and commandments. If you have time to look over them you'll notice how often Jesus issues commands that he fully expects for us to hear, take in and obey. In fact, Jesus goes so far as to say that a person who builds his/her life on his commandments is wise, whereas a person who chooses not to obey his commands is foolish (cf. Matthew chapter 7:24–29). Note too how often Jesus says we are to listen and have ears that hear. All the time! Why? Because life with Jesus and loving Jesus starts with our ears. We listen and he communicates. We hear and obey what he teaches and commands. Over time, obedience works what we've heard down into our heart and it becomes an integral part of who we are.

ON THE OTHER SIDE OF DAY 1:

Parable Principle: Obedience is what we build our life with Jesus on.

Scripture Memory Verse for the Week: *"If you love me, obey my commandments" (John 14:14, NLT).*

Rescued into a Life of Obedience

Questions for Reflection:

1. Do you agree that our tameness in life with Jesus equals living obediently? Why or why not?

2. Do you know the commandments of Jesus? Are you familiar with his voice and what he wants to teach you? If so, are you responding with obedience?

3. How do your feelings help in your life with Jesus? How have they hindered you?

4. We show love through obedience. What's an example of this in your own life?

Taking a Quack at It:

Read Matthew chapters 5–7. Prayerfully hone in on one commandment of Jesus that you've refrained from obeying. Ask Jesus to help you in this area and commit to obedience starting in the present moment.

Day 2: "Sensitive to His Leading"

> *6 Jesus told him, "I am the way, the truth, and the life. No one can come to the Father except through me. 7 If you had really known me, you would know who my Father is. From now on, you do know him and have seen him!"*

Usually when we play "horsey," Molly will stock the trough with whatever items of food she feels I need to eat. The rest of the game is my willingness to follow Molly's leading through the house to get from point A to point B—to the food. For Molly, the goal of a horse's obedience is to be led to the trough where nourishment is given.

Becoming sensitive to Molly's leading is pretty straightforward. Molly takes her pink and "fancy" scarf and wraps it around my neck. She's learned to tie pretty tightly, so just about the time I whinny and neigh in discomfort she eases up on the tension. Once tied with my bridle, Molly then throws her pink fleece blanket over my back. With the saddle in place, Molly gets up on my back and begins to steer me. The steering process is both painful and funny. If I'm going too fast, she'll give a good tug on the scarf. If I need to turn a sharp corner, Molly will pull whichever ear is on the side of the turn to let me know that's the new direction we're going in. Between the tugs and the pulls I've grown sensitive to how Molly leads so I can keep from having too tight a scarf or too sore an ear.

~ ~ ~ ~ ~

Jesus also has a goal for leading us. **He wants to get us from wherever we are to the place of the Father's love where nourishment is given.** How Jesus gets us there is at the heart of the scripture for the day: "I am the way, the truth, and the life. No one can come to the Father except through me" (John 14:6, NLT).

A lot of us take issue with the exclusive nature of this statement. We buck against it. We whinny and neigh in disagreement. *Jesus—the only way? Certainly there are multiple paths to arriving at a life with God!* Yet in making this exclusive statement, Jesus is simply pointing out how the nature of our life with God gets started. There is a relationship and ownership Jesus rightfully has on you and me. His love and teaching are our bit and bridle. His relationship to the Father is what we are invited into, and only Jesus knows the path from point A to point B. He's the only one who can guide us and steer us to where we can never get to by ourselves, because he is the only begotten Son of the Father. The difficulty for us is accepting this reality because it requires two humble stances.

The first humble stance is accepting an eternal reality we have not known or been a part of until now. The Father, Son and Holy Spirit have been in an eternal relationship of divine love. If this is what we are invited into, then it only makes sense that we cannot assume we have any say in how the nature of the relationship with God works. To make assumptions would be a like a horse assuming it can critique the food choices of its loving owner. I don't know about you, but I've never seen a horse utter disgust at a trough (unless it contains wheat-cracker and jelly-bean sandwiches). No, the food is placed there by the owner who's taken the initiative, and the horse is led to and invited to partake of what has already been given. The same goes with our relationship with God. We are invited into a relationship that's already been going on from all of eternity. We come to the trough of this relationship and we participate in what has already been prepared and given. In other

Rescued into a Life of Obedience

words, we don't initiate what relationship with God looks like. We respond to what's being offered in love.

The second humble stance is accepting that Jesus is the only one who knows how to lead us to this relationship. He is the way to the Father. There is no other way or path. When I worked on the horse farm in Kentucky, there was a path that meandered through the woods to the trough outside of the barn. There was one path (I helped create it), and there needed to be no other. There was only one trough for the horses. There was one barn and one stall for each horse. I never looked at the path, trough or barn and thought, "This is way too exclusive! In order for the horses to feel comfortable, why don't we give them options of paths and troughs and barns." No. It made sense to have one of each.

Jesus is the only Son. There is no other and need of no other. He alone knows the path to the Father. As horses, you and I are to humbly accept this reality. We are to follow Jesus' lead. Our ears need to burn a little as we work them in the direction of his teaching and commands. As we do so, we are led to the one Father of all. One place of relational nourishment, where we all become one in community as we are nourished by his love and care. This is freely given. We are called to freely respond as we follow Jesus on the other side of our rescue.

On the Other Side of Day 2:

Parable Principle: Jesus wants to get us from wherever we are to the place of the Father's love where nourishment is given.

Scripture Memory Verse for the Week: *"If you love me, obey my commandments"* (John 14:14, NLT).

Questions for Reflection:

1. Have you ever experienced being led by another person? What was that experience like? What was beneficial? What was hurtful?

2. If Jesus' goal is to lead us to the Father, what does this destination look like for you? Is it one of joy and excitement? Is it one of dread and fear? Why?

3. How have you become sensitive to the leading of Jesus?

4. In what areas of life have you been pursuing your own direction? What have been the results?

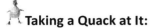
Taking a Quack at It:

Lectio Divina is the discipline of praying with scripture. Take the text for this week and do the following:

- Read through the account twice. Listen for words or phrases that stand out to you.

- Reread the account with your eyes, ears and senses. What do you see? What do you hear? What do you sense?

- Take some time to ponder the passage. Is there an invitation in the account addressed to you? How would this invitation impact your life over the next few days if you were sensitive to the Lord's leading?

DAY 3: "SOUR APPLES"

> 18 "If the world hates you, remember that it hated me first. 19 The world would love you as one of its own if you belonged to it, but you are no longer part of the world. I chose you to come out of the world, so it hates you. 20 Do you remember what I told you? 'A slave is not greater than the master.' Since they persecuted me, naturally they will persecute you. And if they had listened to me, they would listen to you. 21 They will do all this to you because of me, for they have rejected the One who sent me."

When I was a child, I used to go to my Great Grandma Mary's house every Sunday after church to help my grandfather and two older brothers mow and weed her yard, as she was too frail to tend to it herself. Looking back, I can now see the connection I rarely made as a kid. We worshipped the Lord at church and we put our love for Jesus into practice as we served my great grandmother. Although I didn't always enjoy the job at hand, I did enjoy the benefits that came with being at her house. Next to the backyard there were train tracks that supported an active railway schedule; and there was an old work horse that lived in the field the tracks ran through.

The horse was nothing to look at. He resembled my great grandmother's life stage in that he was aging and frail. But what he lacked in his physical presence he more than made up for in his appetite. So I'd walk to the field and watch him from the other side of the fence. Although the old horse was intimidating to me, a small kid, I was bold enough to climb onto the barbed-wire fence and reach up into a nearby crabapple tree. I'd pick quite a few apples and entice the horse to come over and eat out of my hand. He responded each and every time, as the apples I picked off the tree were much more appealing than the countless rotting ones scattered around the base of the tree's trunk.

I loved to listen to the horse eat. He'd eat the apples whole—core, seeds and all. He'd munch and swallow and then come back for more. I used to think the seeds he ate were growing a massive orchard in his belly. I thought his teeth were amazing in their size. I liked the kindness in his old and tired eyes. I liked this horse a lot.

One afternoon when I was feeding the horse, I could hear my own stomach rumbling with hunger. I had mowed the lawn for the better part of two hours and dinner was still an hour or more away. So I thought I'd try the apples the horse seemed so pleased with. I looked for a good candidate in the limbs. I reached up and picked it. Rubbing the skin of the apple on the dry patches of my t-shirt, and seeing no bugs or worm holes, I took as big a bite as I could. I was surprised to find the taste of the apple was way too sour and tart. My lips puckered and there was no one to kiss. My throat hurt and my stomach started to turn. So I spit out what I'd tried to eat and gave the rest of the uneaten apple to the horse. It struck me as rather odd that he and I didn't share the same taste.

~ ~ ~ ~ ~

Just like my experience with that old horse, we soon find that the life of Jesus doesn't suit our taste all that much. Now most of us love to watch Jesus. We like the kindness in his eyes. We even get pretty close to him on a Sunday in worship. With rumbling stomachs itching for lunch, we sit through the service and wonder if our taste buds are similar to those of Jesus'. So when the cue is given, we walk forward and take a piece of the broken bread. Then we take in a small amount of the fruit of the vine. We pray a little, think a little, ponder the meaning of it all, and find that the suffering love of Jesus is something we aren't too sure we can stomach. Suffering is way too sour for our taste! So we leave worship and the Lord's Supper behind as we go after what we do enjoy eating: the acceptance of the people around us.

~ ~ ~ ~ ~

Jesus said, "If the world hates you, remember that it hated me first. The world would love you as one of its own if you belonged to it, but you are no longer part of the world. I chose you to come out of the world, so it hates you. Do you remember what I told you? 'A slave is not greater than the master.' Since they persecuted me, naturally they will persecute you. And if they had listened to me, they would listen to you. They will do all this to you because of me, for they have rejected the One who sent me" (John 15:18–21, NLT).

Take in the significance of these statements. **Jesus is saying that to follow him on the other side of our rescue is to come to a place where we learn to have a taste for the world's hatred.** This isn't a masochistic appetite, it's the willingness to take in and stomach the world's hatred, because we long to be nourished and to live out of the recipes of the Kingdom of Heaven. The recipes of the Kingdom of Heaven are not what the world savors or stomachs. Loving one's enemy is foreign to the taste of this world. Turning the other cheek is way too sour. Going the extra mile... doing to others what you'd have them do to you... serving rather than being served... choosing last place rather than butting into first place... all of these recipes of the Kingdom of Heaven are not the kinds of food this world yearns for. They are sour and disgusting to the taste buds of our success-driven and people-pleasing approaches to life. So if we're going to be nourished at the trough of Jesus' love and be fed these truths and act on them... guess what? We're going to be spit out by this world.

Jesus underscores this reality by saying to you and me that what was true for him will be true for us. "A slave is not greater than the master.' Since they persecuted me, naturally they will persecute you" (John 15:20a, NLT). Have you ever thought of the idea that when we attempt to avoid suffering for Jesus we are really trying to be greater than him? It's impossible to call Jesus my Lord and attempt to live above his sufferings. Rather, Jesus says we have to reframe our appetites. An appetite for the approval of this world is like an appetite for candy bars. It might taste good in the moment, but the end benefit is no nutrition whatsoever. Inevitably we go through the rollercoaster sugar crash. However, developing a taste for the way of Jesus may taste like sour apples at the start, but the end result of obeying Jesus' teachings and manner of life is what brings lasting nourishment and peace. Why? Because as we stomach the world's hatred on account of following Jesus, we eventually come out of this world and into an eternally-close love relationship with our heavenly Father.

Let's look again at the text for the day, "The world would love you as one of its own if you belonged to it, but you are no longer part of the world. I chose you to come out of the world, so it hates you. Do you remember what I told you? 'A slave is not greater than the master.' Since they persecuted me, naturally they will persecute you. And if they had listened to me, they would listen to you. They will do all this to you because of me, for they have rejected the One who sent me" (John 15:19–21, NLT).

Having an appetite for the life of Jesus and the suffering that can come to us as a result is about a relational reality. I belong to Jesus; therefore, I don't belong to this world. Having an appetite for the life of Jesus is making the conscious movement from standing on the barbed-wire fence and reaching over, to joining Jesus on the other side of the fence and developing a taste for what might come across as sour.

ON THE OTHER SIDE OF DAY 3:

Parable Principle: To follow Jesus on the other side of our rescue is to come to a place where we learn to have a taste for the world's hatred.

Scripture Memory Verse for the Week: *"If you love me, obey my commandments" (John 14:14, NLT).*

Questions for Reflection:

1. What does your appetite crave most? What are some foods you can't even begin to stomach?

2. Have you found the life of Jesus to be foreign to your sense of taste? What aspects of this life on the other side of your rescue are hard to stomach? Why?

3. What experiences have you had where your love for Jesus caused those around you to dislike you? What was it like? What did you learn through that experience(s)?

4. What are some ways you've learned to gain strength in living out the life of Jesus in the midst of this world's hatred? What are some of your growing edges?

Taking a Quack at It:

Jesus says we are to pray for those who persecute us (cf. Matthew 5:44). Name those people who dislike you because you love Jesus. Commit to pray for them by name today.

DAY 4: "STAYING AT THE TROUGH"

> 1 "I am the true grapevine, and my Father is the gardener. 2 He cuts off every branch of mine that doesn't produce fruit, and he prunes the branches that do bear fruit so they will produce even more. 3 You have already been pruned and purified by the message I have given you. 4 Remain in me, and I will remain in you. For a branch cannot produce fruit if it is severed from the vine, and you cannot be fruitful unless you remain in me."

I had a difficult time staying at the trough. Wheat-cracker and jelly-bean sandwiches were not pleasant to eat and digest, and my first impulse was to get as far away from Molly's trough as I could. But Molly meant for me to stay. To finish what I'd started. To remain.

There's trouble for a horse that can't stay long enough at the trough to get its needed nourishment. It's a possible sign that something's wrong. You see, most horses with a good appetite will stay and consume what's been offered. Walking away before taking more than a bite or two is sure to mean harm for the hungry horse.

~ ~ ~ ~ ~

The same holds true for our life in Jesus. We've been rescued. We've been placed down into a life of freedom and, as I mentioned in week one, sometimes our assumption is that Jesus has gotten us out of our medians only to shoo us on into a life lived on our own terms. But that's not what the Bible teaches. The Bible tells us that **we've been rescued in order that we can now keep close company with Jesus, who's done**

the rescuing. Putting it simply, we've been rescued for the purpose of relationship. You and I are to stay at the trough of relationship with Jesus, learning to have a taste for what he offers us. We are called to remain.

Take note of the word "in" that's prominent in verse 4. You can't get this sense of closeness with any other preposition. It indicates a place. It signifies where we are to be situated when it comes to relationship with Jesus. The analogy Jesus uses brings this point home. "I am the true grapevine.... Remain in me, and I will remain in you. For a branch cannot produce fruit if it is severed from the vine, and you cannot be fruitful unless you remain in me" (John 15:1a, 4, NLT).

In a very real way, a branch is so closely related to the grapevine that it is "in" it. It's not just situated on the vine, it's connected in such a way that the fibers and life-giving nourishment of the grapevine flow into the branch, causing growth, health and fruit. The jelly-bean flavors in my wheat-cracker and jelly-bean sandwich mimicked the wonderful and vibrant flavors that often issue out of a vine. Grape. Raspberry. Blackberry. These fruits are enjoyed because of the *prepositional* reality of the branch to the vine. "In."

Jesus takes this analogy from the field. He uses this metaphor, which even a horse would have a taste for, and says that what's true of a branch and its vine is to be true of our lives with Jesus. We are to remain in Jesus just like a healthy branch remains in the grapevine.

~ ~ ~ ~ ~

Remaining in Jesus isn't easy. Yesterday we took note of the pain our relationship with Jesus may cause us. At times it's like having to stomach a sour apple or a wheat-cracker and jelly-bean sandwich. Nevertheless, we are to remain. This is a call to perseverance. To remain in Jesus is to go the road of persevering in relationship. Eugene Peterson, one of my favorite authors, defines perseverance as "sticktoittiveness."[1] We stick with our life with Jesus. We hang in there. We remain at the trough.

~ ~ ~ ~ ~

Well over a decade ago I had just begun my journey with Jesus into full-time ministry. I was wide-eyed and the sky was the limit when I thought of what could come of my vocation. With success on my brain, I took the initiative to get with other pastors in the Atlanta area and learn from them the secrets of ministerial success. I couldn't wait to learn and grow.

My first lunch was with a newly retired pastor who had been on staff at a mega-church close to where I worked as an associate pastor. When we sat down to lunch, I simply got the conversation going with the following question, "How would you define success in ministry?" With pen in hand and notebook at the ready, I waited impatiently for what he would share. Yet what he said took me by surprise. Without pausing for a single moment, he looked at me and smiled and said, "That I'm still a Christian after 40 years of ministry is success to me."

I laughed. He didn't.

"No," he said, "I'm serious! Success is being able to get through four decades of full-time ministry and still love Jesus on the other side."

I'll never forget his answer. I assumed there'd be leadership principles and administrative processes that he'd hammer home. I thought there'd be books to read and relationships to leverage. But all he pointed to was the simple fact that he had remained … persevered … stuck with Jesus.

~ ~ ~ ~ ~

Jesus wants us to remain in him. He is the life-source. He's the one who makes us healthy and able to produce anything good in life. Will we situate ourselves in him? Will we stay close and be nourished by him? Will we remain?

On the Other Side of Day 4:

Parable Principle: We've been rescued in order that we can now keep close company with Jesus, who's done the rescuing.

Scripture Memory Verse for the Week: *"If you love me, obey my commandments"* (John 14:14, NLT).

Questions for Reflection:

1. Name some areas in your life where you have remained and persevered. What were the influences that helped you do so?

2. How do you respond to the idea that Jesus has rescued you for the purpose of relationship with him? How is your relationship with Jesus going?
3. Define those times when you've been close to Jesus. How and why do they differ from the ones when you've been far from Jesus?
4. Do you view your daily life with Jesus like a branch related to a grapevine? Why or why not?
5. What would need to change in your life for you to remain "in" Jesus?

Taking a Quack at It:

Ask Jesus to show you where you are in proximity to him. Spend time waiting and listening. If you have wandered far from him, ask him to help you draw close (cf. James 4:8a).

Day 5: "Choices, Choices, Choices"

16 "You didn't choose me. I chose you."

Before the game "horsey" ever got started, Molly had a choice to make. Who would be the horse? Now this wasn't an easy choice. You see, Molly had gotten a ride-on horse for Christmas. This plush play-horse came complete with a saddle, bit and bridle, mane, electronic buttons that make the horse whinny and snort, and a spring-activated system that lets a child actually ride the horse up and down the street. What a gift!

I don't know how or when Molly actually made her choice. I wasn't with her when she did. She didn't consult with me or ask for my input. Molly simply made a choice one day, and the choice was me. Daddy, and not the new Christmas horse (or Mommy, who has much more hair for a mane and would be better suited in pink), would be Molly's choice when it came time to play "horsey."

I have to admit that I've always been flattered by Molly's choice. It's nice to be chosen. It kind of eases the pain of childhood memories when I was one of the last ones to get picked for kickball and dodge ball. All of us, at one time or another, love the experience of being the chosen one.

~ ~ ~ ~ ~

Jesus says, "You didn't choose me. I chose you" (John 15:16, NLT). Ponder this statement. If you need to, go back to the beginning of each of the gospels and read the accounts of how Jesus called the twelve to himself. It's pretty clear; the disciples didn't choose Jesus. He chose them.

What changes in our dynamic with Jesus when we consider the truth that he chose us and we didn't choose him? Who's the initiator? Where is the onus of relationship? Sometimes it's easy to assume that we choose Jesus. The day I decided to follow Jesus. The time I accepted Jesus into my heart. These assumptions and more like them lead us to believe that life with Jesus is because of what we have done. We need to rethink this assumption. Jesus has chosen us. In fancy terminology we call this prevenient grace. Prevenient grace is the love of God that quite literally goes before us. We are unaware. We are helplessly ignorant. Nevertheless, God goes before us. Lovingly, he sees us, takes notice, takes time, reaches out and rescues.

Many Christians throughout the ages have come to the conviction that even our ability to respond to the Lord's rescuing love is a gift of grace. So in a sense, **our entire rescue, including any response we might take ownership for, is God's gift, God's work, God's choice of us**. God is everywhere the initiator. We have only to humbly respond. He chooses us. We gratefully recognize that we've been chosen. Further, we need to own the fact that when God chooses us, he also chooses all of creation through us.

Romans 8:19 says, "...all of creation is waiting eagerly for that future day when God will reveal who his children really are." Ponder this. All of creation is waiting with bated breath. All of creation is bound up in God's rescue of you and me. So when we read about God's life with his people, we notice that when God came to Moses, he really came close to all of Moses' kin. When God rescued Israel, he began the rescue operation for all the nations through this people who were once not a people at all. When Jesus called the twelve, he began to call all of us as he sent them out to make disciples of all the nations (cf. Matthew 28:19). God has chosen you and me—and through us God chooses all of us. We respond.

We go. We share the good news. We tell others the incredible truth that even though they may pale in comparison to a new Christmas horse, they have been intentionally chosen by a God of limitless love.

On the Other Side of Day 5:

Parable Principle: Our entire rescue, including any response we might take ownership for, is God's gift, God's work, God's choice of us.

Scripture Memory Verse for the Week: *"If you love me, obey my commandments" (John 14:14, NLT).*

Questions for Reflection:

1. Think of a time when you were NOT chosen by your peers. What did that experience do to you in that moment?
2. Think of a time when you were chosen. What does that memory mean to you?
3. Why is it easy to take the initiative for our life in Jesus? Do you agree that believing we have initiated relationship with Jesus compromises our life with God? Why or why not?
4. Do you believe God has intentionally chosen you? If so, what is your inner response?
5. Are you willing to go and share the good news that God has chosen all of creation to experience his love? Why or why not?

Taking a Quack at It:

Celebration is the way we worship the Lord. Make a point to enter worship this week with a desire to respond with gratitude for all that the Lord has done in your life.

Day 6: "Girth"

> 26 "...I will send you the Advocate—the Spirit of truth. He will come to you from the Father and will testify all about me. 27 And you

must also testify about me because you have been with me from the beginning of my ministry."

When a saddle is placed on the back of a horse, there's an important strap that cinches the saddle to the underside of the horse. This is so that the rider can ride without falling off of the horse's back. It's called a girth. Without a well-fit girth, most riders would fall off a trotting or running horse and injure themselves. A girth protects against this danger.

When Molly saddles me, she doesn't have the use of a girth, so there have been times when I've started ambling through the house and she's started to fall off my back. Fortunately, she's so petite that she's easy to catch. She laughs and I remind her to sit squarely so she doesn't get hurt. But most times it's a kind of start-and-stop process of Molly riding through the house on my back.

~ ~ ~ ~ ~

It's easy to fall off of following Jesus. We've looked at how life with Jesus on the other side of our rescue is a path of suffering love. At first we tend to saddle up with excitement and great intention, but over time we usually get pretty sore and tired. We can become disillusioned, resentful or even downright tired of this life with Jesus. We lose courage and we often fall off.

~ ~ ~ ~ ~

When I was in my doctoral program at Asbury Theological Seminary, I decided to write my dissertation on the role of courage in effective pastoral ministry and leadership. One of the surprising truths I came across was in the field of military literature. I learned how courage typically diminishes the longer a person is on the battlefield. I had always assumed the opposite. Hollywood-style Rambo, Clint Eastwood and John Wayne always led me to believe that the more battle-seasoned a person, the more courageous their presence. Yet study after study shows how soldiers who face battle and the horrors of the front line get less and less courageous over time. Battle-weariness, shellshock, PTSD and a host of other realities leave combatants exhausted and fearful.

The same can hold true in our life with Jesus. As we walk the path of suffering love, there comes over time a loss of intention and fortitude. Jesus' disciples are a prime example of this reality. They traveled with

Rescued into a Life of Obedience

Jesus for three years. Certainly they experienced a lot of wonderful miracles and life-changing stories. Yet they also increasingly encountered difficulties and hardships as the path to Jerusalem led them into the hatred of the religious elite and the Roman leaders. Fear mounted. Dissension among the twelve increased. Concern over Jesus' suffering and pitiable death loomed larger and larger. As the road became more treacherous, so too did the disciples' ability to stay with Jesus. Battle wearied, each and every one of them deserted Jesus. The saddles of their devotion shifted and fell. They couldn't stay with Jesus.

~ ~ ~ ~ ~

Jesus knows how easily we can fall out of our devotion to him, so he's given us a girth. "I will send you the Advocate—the Spirit of truth. He will come to you from the Father and will testify all about me" (John 15:26, NLT). **The person and presence of the Holy Spirit cinches our life to Jesus' life.** If you look at verse 26 in the original Greek, you'll note that the Holy Spirit is referred to literally as the comforter. I've always thought of this as the comforting presence of God that consoles us in our battle-wearied state; a kind of nursemaid who tends to our wounds and eases our pains. But that's not the point. Remember the girth. Think of being cinched tightly to Jesus. That's the work and presence of the Holy Spirit. He comforts with the purpose of encouraging and emboldening you and me to continue on the path of discipleship in light of our pain and suffering. The Holy Spirit is the girth of courage who cinches us to the life of Jesus.

Makes sense, doesn't it? Just take a cursory look at the Book of Acts, and you'll read account after account of Jesus' followers who were emboldened to bear witness to Jesus despite the abuse and hatred being heaped on them. It's not because they had the strength in and of themselves. It's because the Holy Spirit filled them and cinched them to the life of Jesus. They were *en-couraged* to bear witness.

~ ~ ~ ~ ~

You may be on a saddle of discipleship, but are you cinched? If not, you won't stay on the saddle long. Expect to fall and get hurt. However, if you receive Jesus' promise of the presence of the Holy Spirit, He will cinch you to the life of Jesus. He'll comfort you for the purpose of en-couraging you to testify about Jesus. Jesus said, "You must also testify about me because you have been with me from the beginning of my ministry" (John 15:27, NLT). The Holy Spirit is our girth in our ability to testify about Jesus.

Testifying about Jesus involves words, but is not limited to them. To testify means we reflect a life that is cinched to Jesus' life in both the areas of what we do and what we choose not to do (engagement and abstention). We do this is by obeying his commands. As we obey his commands, we bear witness to Jesus by allowing his truth regarding daily life to show itself in and through us. Painful? Yes. Joyful? Yes! The pain and joy we can experience and endure as we rely on the Holy Spirit to keep us close to the presence of Jesus.

ON THE OTHER SIDE OF DAY 6:

Parable Principle: The person and presence of the Holy Spirit cinches our life to Jesus' life.

Scripture Memory Verse for the Week: *"If you love me, obey my commandments" (John 14:14, NLT).*

Questions for Reflection:

1. If you've ever ridden a horse, what's your experience been like?

2. Would you agree that it's impossible to stay in this life with Jesus in our own strength? Why or why not?

3. Spend some time thinking about the areas of your life, in which you are battle-weary right now. Is there a recurring pattern to this?

4. How does the idea of the Holy Spirit cinching you to the life of Jesus strike you? Have you found this to be true?

5. How have you testified about Jesus in your own life? Getting at this same question another way, how would others know you are a rescued follower of Jesus by the way you live your daily life?

Taking a Quack at It:

In a culture that emphasizes initiative and aggression, this challenge might be tough for you. Nevertheless, spend 10–15 minutes in bed in the coming morning with an intention to be completely passive. Let this show up in your posture. Lie still with palms wide open. Simply pray: "Lord, I give up all control today. I am yours. In every relationship, decision, conversation, activity, I lay myself at your complete disposal. Put me where you will. Use me or put me aside. Lift me up or humble me. I want to be as light as a feather in your hands as I follow you wherever you lead. Amen."

DAY 7: REST

Worship in community.

Enjoy the presence of loved ones.

Take time to take note of God's creation.

Reflect on this past week.

Commit this coming week to the Lord.

ENDNOTE

1. Eugene Peterson, *A Long Obedience in the Same Direction*. Downers Grove, IL: InterVarsity Press, 2000, p. 125.

PARABLE 3

Four-Eyed Gator:
Rescued into a Life of Relinquishment

When we got to the edge of the river, I began to scope out the nearby area. There was a rumor that a 16-foot gator had been seen close to where we were planning to fish, and it had gotten a good piece of a Labrador Retriever's hind leg just a couple of weeks earlier. I was certain the same gator was going to enjoy having me for lunch, so I was panning for the reptile with my polarized eyes. Although I didn't see anything, I was certain it was lurking just below the surface of the water.

The place we had chosen to fish was perfect! There was a low-hanging cypress tree with a massive branch that hung out over the river. Just the kind of seat for a father and a son to fish off of. Getting close to the branch, I thought I'd take an extra look into the water before inviting Chat to come up with me. As I leaned over to look into the murky river, the pair of glasses I had put in my shirt's front pocket slipped out and fell into the water. I lunged as it fell, but I wasn't quick enough. Splash! I watched the silvery metallic frame sink down into the black water. I began to wonder if this was it; if an inextricable force was beckoning me closer to the river where I'd be dragged under by the huge gator.

Although my glasses were just a mere foot into the water, I was too nervous to reach for them. All I could think of were countless pictures of thrashing gators rolling their victims to their miserable deaths. I couldn't risk it. I didn't want to go that way with my son looking on. Fortunately, I remembered that Chat had brought his fishing net along. So I walked up the bank and grabbed the net. I extended the handle and moved the net over my glasses thinking I'd just scoop them up. I quickly turned the net under the sandy bottom of the river and went for the glasses. But I didn't get them. I simply pushed them further into the river. I began to sweat. *I can't afford to lose this pair! Can I wear sunglasses at night? Wasn't there a song about that?* I tried the net a second time, but I was a little distracted. I was trying to keep one eye on the glasses and another on any potential threat further out in the river. I missed again, pushing the glasses further into the riverbed and down a sloping decline. Before I knew it, my glasses had taken a watery ride into the even darker recesses of a hollowed-out palm tree stump submerged under the water.

By this time Chatham was busy fishing. He must've wondered what was keeping me, so he called out, "Hey, dad! You almost done?" I answered, "Be there in a minute, Chat. I have one more thing to try." I was pacing back and forth along the river's edge. I couldn't see my glasses, and I couldn't believe that I'd have to get a new pair. *This is ridiculous! A cell phone last year and now a pair of glasses... there must be a happy Mr. Limpet somewhere under those waters!* As I pondered what to do, I decided to use my new fishing rod to get at my glasses. Although I couldn't see into the hollowed-out palm tree stump, I was sure I could reach into the darkness with my fishing pole, snag the glasses and pull them out. I pushed the pole into the darkness. I scraped and scratched. I pulled out the pole and had hooked nothing. I tried again... and again... and again... each time losing more confidence. They were gone. I'd have to get a new pair. After about an hour of working to get the glasses out of the stump, I heard a loud snap! The end of my new fishing pole had broken off. *Definitely a fish-pole-eating gator lives down in there!*

In desperation I decided I'd be willing to risk sticking my hand into the darkness. The last time I had found myself in a similar situation was as a kid off of a dare (a double-dog one). So I rolled up my sleeve and, although everything in me said not to, I reached into the darkness of the palm tree stump. I felt around the entrance of the stump for a few moments and sensed nothing. Frustrated, I began to reach a little more into the darkness. The further I went, the more my mind began to race. Images of deep-sea monsters with gnashing teeth and terrifying bulbous eyes began to fill my mind. Leeches and horrid-looking water bugs, poisonous snakes and piranha, everything ugly, noxious, and hideous crept into my imagination and captured it. As I became more nervous, I also became less and less willing to go any deeper into what I couldn't see. The darkness was just too dark. Defeated, I pulled my hand back and counted my fingers. I remember feeling an overwhelming desire to be able to see in the dark. Accepting my limitations, I finally decided to head home. As we were walking away, I said to Chat, "Whatever gator lives in the darkness of that river now has 20/20 vision." He laughed and said, "Good times, Dad. Good times." I wasn't convinced.

Biblical Text for Week 3: Matthew 16:13–17:13

[Matthew 16] 13 When Jesus came to the region of Caesarea Philippi, he asked his disciples, "Who do people say that the Son of Man is?"

14 "Well," they replied, "some say John the Baptist, some say Elijah, and others say Jeremiah or one of the other prophets."

15 Then he asked them, "But who do you say I am?"

16 Simon Peter answered, "You are the Messiah, the Son of the living God."

17 Jesus replied, "You are blessed, Simon son of John, because my Father in heaven has revealed this to you. You did not learn this from any human being. 18 Now I say to you that you are Peter (which means 'rock'), and upon this rock I will build my church, and all the powers of hell will not conquer it. 19 And I will give you the keys of the Kingdom of Heaven. Whatever you forbid on earth will be forbidden in heaven, and whatever you permit on earth will be permitted in heaven."

20 Then he sternly warned the disciples not to tell anyone that he was the Messiah.

21 From then on Jesus began to tell his disciples plainly that it was necessary for him to go to Jerusalem, and that he would suffer many terrible things at the hands of the elders, the leading priests, and the teachers of religious law. He would be killed, but on the third day he would be raised from the dead.

22 But Peter took him aside and began to reprimand him for saying such things. "Heaven forbid, Lord," he said. "This will never happen to you!"

23 Jesus turned to Peter and said, "Get away from me, Satan! You are a dangerous trap to me. You are seeing things merely from a human point of view, not from God's."

24 Then Jesus said to his disciples, "If any of you wants to be my follower, you must turn from your selfish ways, take up your cross, and follow me. 25 If you try to hang on to your life, you will lose it. But if you give up your life for my sake, you will save it. 26 And what do you benefit if you gain the whole world but lose your own soul? Is anything worth more than your soul? 27 For the Son of Man will come with his angels in the glory of his Father and will judge all people according to their deeds. 28 And I tell you the truth, some standing here right now will not die before they see the Son of Man coming in his Kingdom."

[Matthew 17] 1 Six days later Jesus took Peter and the two brothers, James and John, and led them up a high mountain to be alone. 2 As the men watched, Jesus' appearance was transformed so that his face shone like the sun, and his clothes became as white as light. 3 Suddenly, Moses and Elijah appeared and began talking with Jesus.

4 Peter exclaimed, "Lord, it's wonderful for us to be here! If you want, I'll make three shelters as memorials—one for you, one for Moses, and one for Elijah."

5 But even as he spoke, a bright cloud overshadowed them, and a voice from the cloud said, "This is my dearly loved Son, who brings me great joy. Listen to him." 6 The disciples were terrified and fell face down on the ground.

7 Then Jesus came over and touched them. "Get up," he said. "Don't be afraid." 8 And when they looked up, Moses and Elijah were gone, and they saw only Jesus.

9 As they went back down the mountain, Jesus commanded them, "Don't tell anyone what you have seen until the Son of Man has been raised from the dead."

10 Then his disciples asked him, "Why do the teachers of religious law insist that Elijah must return before the Messiah comes?"

11 Jesus replied, "Elijah is indeed coming first to get everything ready. 12 But I tell you, Elijah has already come, but he wasn't recognized, and they chose to abuse him. And in the same way they will also make the

Rescued into a Life of Relinquishment

Son of Man suffer." 13 Then the disciples realized he was talking about John the Baptist.

Day 1: "Polarized"

13 When Jesus came to the region of Caesarea Philippi, he asked his disciples, "Who do people say that the Son of Man is?"

14 "Well," they replied, "some say John the Baptist, some say Elijah, and others say Jeremiah or one of the other prophets."

15 Then he asked them, "But who do you say I am?"

16 Simon Peter answered, "You are the Messiah, the Son of the living God."

17 Jesus replied, "You are blessed, Simon son of John, because my Father in heaven has revealed this to you. You did not learn this from any human being. 18 Now I say to you that you are Peter (which means 'rock'), and upon this rock I will build my church, and all the powers of hell will not conquer it. 19 And I will give you the keys of the Kingdom of Heaven. Whatever you forbid on earth will be forbidden in heaven, and whatever you permit on earth will be permitted in heaven."

20 Then he sternly warned the disciples not to tell anyone that he was the Messiah.

Polarized sunglasses give me clarity of vision. When Chatham and I head out to fish at the ocean's edge, at a local pond or down by the Econ River, I always find that having polarized lenses helps me see what I normally couldn't without them. They help my eyes cut through the top of the water and see down into where the fish (and gators) are hanging out. Although I've had my pair of sunglasses for a couple of years now, they always feel like a brand new gift when I put them on to go fishing.

In our text for today we read of a time when Peter was wearing polarized lenses of faith. He normally didn't see things so crystal clear, but on this particular day he could see with remarkable accuracy. It must have been a gift to see so well, because when Jesus asked the all important question, Peter was able to see what the other disciples couldn't. Let's take a look at the text again.

"'Who do people say that the Son of Man is?'

'Well,' they replied, 'some say John the Baptist, some say Elijah, and others say Jeremiah or one of the other prophets.' Then he asked them, 'But who do you say I am?' Simon Peter answered, 'You are the Messiah, the Son of the living God'" (Matthew 16:13–16, NLT).

~ ~ ~ ~

We had been fishing for hours off the pier at Cocoa Beach. None of us had caught a thing. Pastor Joe hadn't, my father-in-law hadn't, my son hadn't, and neither had I. We were ready to head home. Our necks were not only sunburned, they were also sore from craning over the pier and into the inlet waters. But Chatham wasn't ready to go. He had one last piece of shrimp and he was certain he could catch whatever fish was nibbling on his line. I walked over to him. To be honest, I was a little impatient.

"Come on, Chat, there's nothing down there. Let's get going. We're all tired."

He wouldn't have anything of it. "No, dad! There's a fish coming out of the rock, and I'm gonna get it. Just give me a minute. I'm sure I can see it and it looks hungry!"

I sighed. I didn't look forward to his hopes getting let down, but I knew there just wasn't anything biting. Just when I was going to say that we really needed to get going, Chatham let out a scream of excitement. I saw his fishing pole bow out. There was something on his line! I dropped the tackle and got closer to Chatham as he reeled it in. I couldn't believe it... there came up and out of the water a fascinating catch. A black and white striped Sheepshead. It weighed a good four pounds, and Chat could hardly contain himself.

"See, Dad! I told you I could get it! I told you I saw something!" He hopped up and down in disbelief of his amazing catch.

We marveled at the Sheepshead. The smooth rows of white teeth. The coloration. The fact that Chat had made the only catch of the day. Pastor Joe filleted the fish and we put it on ice. Chat enjoyed fresh fish for dinner.

~ ~ ~ ~

Like my experience with Chatham, the disciples didn't see what Peter saw the day Jesus asked them about his identity. They saw a gifted but ordinary man. They saw someone perhaps on par with John the Baptist or an Old Testament legend. But not Peter. Peter had eyes to see something more. When the disciples grew tired of the conversation, Peter remained at the water's edge peering in. He knew something more was there for the taking. It was there, biting at the tip of his tongue. It was there, just out of reach of what he could put his finger on. But then—just when the others were ready to retire—it came to him at the last moment: "You are the Messiah, the Son of the living God" (Matthew 16:16, NLT). They marveled at Peter's catch of faith. The sheer uniqueness of it was a wonder to behold.

Like the gift of polarized lenses, Peter's insight into Jesus' identity was a gift. Jesus said, "my Father in heaven has revealed this to you. You did not learn this from any human being" (Matthew 16:17, NLT).

Jesus' words to Peter remind us that our ability to see the truth of Jesus is not of our own making. We cannot use our own eyes to see it. However, if we're willing to stay long enough at the water's edge, waiting with the hope of a child, God will honor our faithfulness and enable us to see clearly what we hadn't been able to perceive before.

The ability to see Jesus for who he is comes to us as a gift. Like a new pair of polarized sunglasses on a fishing trip, the Father gives us eyes of faith to see what most can't. What this does on the other side of our rescue is it keeps us both humble and faithful. Humble because we're not smart enough to think up the truth of Jesus on our own; and faithful because we receive from the Father this gift of faith and we turn to him in prayer asking that others would receive as we have.

The challenge for most comes in this: Are we willing to stay at the water's edge? Are we willing to intentionally look when most have retired, because they're too sore to stick around with us? Are we willing to be like Chatham was that day at the pier—faithful, hopeful, certain that there was a catch to be had, and rejoicing when it came as we looked on with amazement? I hope so because I'll tell you this, watching Chat catch a fish made me want to head back to the water myself and stay longer than I would have. I guess I'm glad that the faith of a child far exceeds the cynicism of a tired and sore fisherman like me.

On the Other Side of Day 1:

Parable Principle: The ability to see Jesus for who he is comes to us as a gift.

Scripture Memory Verse for the Week: *"If you try to hang on to your life, you will lose it. But if you give up your life for my sake, you will save it"* (Matthew 16:25, NLT).

Questions for Reflection:

1. Do you have the faith of a child to stay by the water's edge? Why or why not?
2. When was the last time you saw Jesus clearly? Describe that experience.
3. Do you agree that the ability to see Jesus for who he really is comes to a person as a gift? Why or why not?
4. Like my son's willingness to stick it out to catch a fish, perseverance is essential in the life of faith. How have you experienced this yourself?
5. How has the faith of a child affected the way you look at Jesus?

Taking a Quack at It:

Take time today to thank your heavenly Father for the way he has loved you. Be authentic as you consider the love behind why he has led you to Jesus. If you have not come to a certain faith in the truth of Jesus, simply ask the Father to reveal Jesus to you. Ask him to help you see clearly. Then wait.

Day 2: "Black-Water Tributary"

> *21 From then on Jesus began to tell his disciples plainly that it was necessary for him to go to Jerusalem, and that he would suffer many terrible things at the hands of the elders, the leading priests, and the teachers of religious law. He would be killed, but on the third day he*

would be raised from the dead. 22 But Peter took him aside and began to reprimand him for saying such things. "Heaven forbid, Lord," he said. "This will never happen to you!"

Jesus' disciples have been rescued. They have been called out of their former life and into a new life with Jesus. So there they are, traveling along, and everything appears bright and clear. Jesus has just asked what the disciples believe about him and Peter's nailed it! Jesus is none other than the Son of the living God. The disciples are ecstatic! The world's for the taking and they are close to the one who's due everything. But rather than relish the truth of Jesus and remain in an elevated state of relief and safety, Jesus takes them where they least expect to go: the black waters of his looming suffering and death.

"Jesus began to tell his disciples plainly that it was necessary for him to go to Jerusalem, and that he would suffer many terrible things at the hands of the elders, the leading priests, and the teachers of religious law. He would be killed..." (Matthew 16:21, NLT).

Can you imagine how the disciple's mouths must have gone completely slack? They are bewildered, stumped, confused, doubtful, suspicious, even downright angry! "But Peter took him aside and began to reprimand him for saying such things. 'Heaven forbid, Lord,' he said. 'This will never happen to you!'" (Matthew 16:22, NLT).

Like Peter, we often want to reprimand Jesus. We want to forbid the life of Jesus from being the way it is. We can certainly be grateful that he's rescued us, and we can even become familiar with the journey of suffering love Jesus travels; however, we struggle with journeying with him. Suffering? No way! Rejection? Not on your life! Humility? Not when success and acclaim can be had! We just don't like the path of Jesus. We want the crystal-clear river version of faith, not the murky black-river tributary. Nevertheless, to follow Jesus means there can be pain. There are things lurking under the water that might just get a good chunk out of you if they can. Why? Because the purposes of God have to be accomplished in the very dark and sinful realities of the people he's come to rescue. If we're going to keep company with him, we've got to get used to the darkness as well.

~ ~ ~ ~ ~

Several months ago I was startled to see three warts beginning to grow on my hands. I've never had warts before, and it was pretty embarrassing because my job is a people-centered job. I shake a lot of hands and meet with a lot of people. So I was self-conscious, embarrassed, worried. I didn't want people to see my warts. They were ugly and painful, and pastors aren't supposed to have them. (Remember the old adage, "cleanliness is next to godliness"? I guess I made the assumption around this.) So after exhausting the over-the-counter options, which didn't work for me, I decided to go to my doctor.

We have a really good and loving doctor. She's treated both me and my wife for the last four years, and we've grown to respect her a lot. It was kind of funny. Although she sees most people "warts and all," I wanted to hide them even from her. But she poked some good humor at me and brought levity to my embarrassment. When I finally thought it was safe, I put my hands out for her to see and examine the warts. After taking a look at them, she took some freezing agent and applied it directly onto my warts. After just a few treatments they were gone.

~ ~ ~ ~

If my doctor treats the infection at the source, isn't the same true of Jesus? Jesus didn't come to remedy our sin by living comfortably by a quiet and scenic river. No! Jesus came to address our warts by entering into the very source of our sinful, broken, hate-filled and murderous realities. Jesus journeyed into the black-water tributary of this world's sin, and no amount of forbidding or reprimanding can change the path of Jesus' suffering love.

Jesus has rescued us. Jesus has called us to follow him. **As we follow Jesus a bend or two down the path, we learn that Jesus leads us to the black-water tributaries of suffering love**. We don't like the spot. It's not the kind of place we'd choose ourselves. It lacks amenities and it's a different kind of place than where the world tends to go. We feel alone. We feel like we're missing out. We aren't comfortable watching Jesus suffer. The shadow of the cross is more the norm than the shadow of a passing billowy cloud on a sunny afternoon. This is Good Friday kind of stuff and we're not pleased. But Jesus is. Jesus is pleased because it's in this very place that his light—his remedy—can come into the darkness and begin to heal.

Rescued into a Life of Relinquishment

ON THE OTHER SIDE OF DAY 2:

Parable Principle: As we follow Jesus a bend or two down the path, we learn that he leads us to the black-water tributaries of suffering love.

Scripture Memory Verse for the Week: *"If you try to hang on to your life, you will lose it. But if you give up your life for my sake, you will save it"* (Matthew 16:25, NLT).

Questions for Reflection:

1. What are some places you've been that were far from scenic and lovely? What were those experiences like?

2. Ponder Jesus' words in Matthew 16 and reflect on Peter's reaction. How would you have responded/reacted to Jesus? Would you have struggled like Peter? Why?

3. To what dark areas of your sin has Jesus applied his remedy? Are there areas of your life where you've been afraid to show Jesus your warts? If so, why?

4. What does walking with Jesus to the black-water tributary look like in your life right now? How might it look in the future?

Taking a Quack at It:

The song, "Where He Leads Me"[1], is a powerful hymn I used to sing in church as a child. Ponder these simple verses today:

> I can hear my Savior calling,
> I can hear my Savior calling,
> I can hear my Savior calling,
> "Take thy cross and follow, follow Me."
>
> Where He leads me I will follow,
> Where He leads me I will follow,
> Where He leads me I will follow;
> I'll go with Him, with Him, all the way.
>
> I'll go with Him through the garden,
> I'll go with Him through the garden,

I'll go with Him through the garden,
I'll go with Him, with Him all the way.

I'll go with Him through the judgment,
I'll go with Him through the judgment,
I'll go with Him through the judgment,
I'll go with Him, with Him all the way.

He will give me grace and glory,
He will give me grace and glory,
He will give me grace and glory,
And go with me, with me all the way.

Day 3: "Deadliest Catch"

> *21 From then on Jesus began to tell his disciples plainly that it was necessary for him to go to Jerusalem, and that he would suffer many terrible things at the hands of the elders, the leading priests, and the teachers of religious law. He would be killed, but on the third day he would be raised from the dead.*
>
> *22 But Peter took him aside and began to reprimand him for saying such things. "Heaven forbid, Lord," he said. "This will never happen to you!"*
>
> *23 Jesus turned to Peter and said, "Get away from me, Satan! You are a dangerous trap to me. You are seeing things merely from a human point of view, not from God's."*

Chatham and I love to watch the show *Deadliest Catch*. It's a reality show about crab fisherman who brave treacherous waters and risk their lives to catch crab in the Bering Sea. Sometimes the show inspires us to try some new fishing techniques of our own. So one day we built our own crab trap. Now it wasn't for salt water crab, but it was for fresh water crab... well... ok... it was for crawfish. We built a trap to catch pond-dwelling crawfish.

We had it all mapped out. We took an empty plastic coffee can and cut a small opening on either end. We placed a piece of salmon inside the "trap." Chat had some thin rope which we attached to the can and, after filling the base of the can with some rocks, we threw the trap into the pond, tied the rope around the tree and spent the night dreaming of a massive catch of crawfish. After school the next day, Chat and I raced out to the pond. We pulled the trap in and looked to see what we had caught. Nothing! Not one crawfish, minnow or pond-dwelling critter! Although we didn't catch crawfish, we're still determined to make a trap that will catch something one of these days. But the traps the fisherman use in the show *Deadliest Catch* are deadly. They use bait to lure the crabs, traps to catch the crabs, and holds in the ships to carry the crabs to port and eventually to market.

~ ~ ~ ~ ~

In our text for the day we learn how Peter was a deadly trap to Jesus. Jesus shared with the disciples the path he would travel to a black-water tributary of suffering and death. Peter couldn't stand the thought and so he stammered out that no such future could possibly await this Son of the living God. Peter even went so far as to say, "Heaven forbid it, Lord" (Matthew 16:22, NLT). Peter was in essence baiting Jesus. He was asking Jesus to take the bite of a future that held no suffering or death.

If offered the same bait, you and I would undoubtedly go after it. Without a second thought, we'd take the bait and not think twice. It's a part of our culture of comfort. Recent studies show that an attitude of self-centeredness is on the increase. Young people feel less and less empathy for the pain and suffering of others. We have been baited and drawn into a belief that the best kind of life is a life lived without suffering love. We don't want it and we don't particularly want to come alongside those who are hurting.

Jesus sees this bait of a painless future for what it really is: a deadly trap. "Get away from me, Satan! You are a dangerous trap to me. You are seeing things merely from a human point of view, not from God's" (Matthew 16:23, NLT).

When we approach our life on the other side of our rescue from a human point of view, we are in the act of setting a deadly trap for the life of Jesus. Our pursuit of avoiding the black-water tributaries is a deadly trap. There is no remedy or healing with avoidance. Our desire for comfort and love to be painless is a deadly trap. Greater love, according to Jesus, is the act of laying one's life down for one's friend. Our lust for the approval of others is a deadly trap. Jesus was despised and rejected. Our hatred of an enemy is a deadly trap. Jesus told us to forgive and to pray for those who persecute us. Our desire for more and more material stuff is a deadly trap. Jesus said we cannot serve two masters. Our concern over the needs of tomorrow is a deadly trap. Jesus said no amount of worry can ever add a single moment to our lives.

At every turn, the human point of view is a deadly trap to the life of Jesus. The bait may be alluring. We may be hungry. But if we follow our own world's way of thinking, living and relating, we miss the way God thinks, lives and relates. So what we need to become is "cross-eyed." We need to accept the cross of Jesus that is at the center of our life in him. If we follow Jesus, we will inevitably have to do a lot of cross-carrying. According to Jesus, we must lose the approach to life with Jesus that assumes I can have Jesus and still take the bait of this world.

Beware of becoming a trap to the life of Jesus! Check your desires with the teachings and life of Jesus. Where there are differences, throw away the world's point of view and cling to Jesus. He won't trap you. Jesus will lead you to freedom, and to real and lasting life.

ON THE OTHER SIDE OF DAY 3:

Parable Principle: We must lose the approach to life with Jesus that assumes I can have Jesus and still take the bait of this world.

Scripture Memory Verse for the Week: *"If you try to hang on to your life, you will lose it. But if you give up your life for my sake, you will save it"* (Matthew 16:25, NLT).

Questions for Reflection:

1. Have you ever experienced watching a loved one or friend go through difficulty and suffering? What was the result of their pain? How did it impact you?

2. What do you think or feel about the idea that our initial reaction to the life of Jesus is more than likely a trap for the way of Jesus?

3. How have you learned to see things from God's point of view rather than a human point of view?

4. Are there decisions or realities you're facing that are forcing a choice between God's path and a worldly path? If so, what are those decisions and where are you in relationship to them?

5. What would help you to see things from God's point of view?

Taking a Quack at It:

Discernment can be an important discipline in the life of faith. Danny Morris' book, *Discerning God's Will Together: A Spiritual Practice for the Church*[2], is perhaps one of the best resources on how a community of faith can intentionally discern where the Lord is leading. For our purposes, I want to share one aspect of the discernment process Morris talks about in his book. It's called "shedding."

Shedding is an old Quaker process where a person takes time to reflect on what personal agendas or underlying ambitions he/she might have. It's the willingness to take a good, hard and candid look at oneself with the purpose of discerning what is "of self" and what is "of God." Sometimes the process of shedding can take a good amount of time or require the help of a trusted friend to get at core, self-centered agendas. Once a person understands what thier agendas are, then it becomes their responsibility to confess them and walk away from them... to shed them.

Take some time today to consider what you're facing in your life and where the Lord is calling you. Are their areas you need to do some shedding in? If so, what agendas do you have that are causing you to resist the path of Jesus? Confess it to Jesus, and ask him to help you see things from his point of view.

Day 4: "Lesser Things"

> 24 "...Jesus said to his disciples, "If any of you wants to be my follower, you must turn from your selfish ways, take up your cross, and follow me. 25 If you try to hang on to your life, you will lose it. But if you give up your life for my sake, you will save it. 26 And what do you benefit if you gain the whole world but lose your own soul? Is anything worth more than your soul? 27 For the Son of Man will

come with his angels in the glory of his Father and will judge all people according to their deeds. 28 And I tell you the truth, some standing here right now will not die before they see the Son of Man coming in his Kingdom."

When Chat and I went fishing, I wanted to spend time with him, but that's not what played out. The glasses fell into the water, and I became distracted with trying to get them. The time I had planned to spend with Chatham became time wasted on trying to keep my pair of glasses. As I looked back on that time later in the day, I regretted that I had not been able to put aside my attempts to get the glasses in order to spend the afternoon fishing with my son. I wasted the fishing trip, and guilt settled in. I lost both things—my glasses and the ability to make an afternoon memory with my nine-year-old.

I often see this same exact scenario played out in the lives of people who want to follow Jesus, but who are constantly distracted by lesser things. My dad is a prime example. He's been dead for more than six years now, and his life was the definition of a person pursuing lesser things. He pursued women, alcohol, gambling and money. He went after these distractions; and by the time he was into his early sixties, he had been distracted for so many years that he couldn't help but choose lesser things. Although I shared Jesus' love with him several years before his fatal heart attack, Dad wasn't able to respond.

Jesus understands our human condition. He knows that when we pursue our own version of my pair of glasses at the expense of something infinitely greater, over time we cannot help but do so. We become a part of those lesser things. That's why Jesus says, "If any of you wants to be my follower, you must turn from your selfish ways, take up your cross, and follow me. If you try to hang on to your life, you will lose it. But if you give up your life for my sake, you will save it. And what do you benefit if you gain the whole world but lose your own soul? Is anything worth more than your soul" (Matthew 16:24–26, NLT)?

What Jesus is getting at is the tension I felt at the Econ River. I wanted to hang onto my glasses. I didn't want to see them go. But there was Chatham fishing solo. I wasn't by his side. I wasn't talking with him and listening to him. I couldn't see what he was baiting his line with or take time to point out where the fish might be hanging out. We didn't laugh together, and I didn't hear how his day at school had gone. Now you might consider this example as making a big deal out of a moment in time that isn't all that significant. But think again. You see, in that minor incident I chose what I would never gain over a relationship I could have had. Take a moment to ponder this principle. I chose what I could never gain over a relationship I could have had. That's what Jesus is saying. He's saying that if we try to hang onto our lives at the expense of following him, we're choosing what we can never gain over a relationship we could have with him. We lose out twice.

To choose Jesus is to turn away from our selfish ways. "If any of you wants to be my follower, you must turn from your selfish ways, take up your cross and follow me" (Matthew 16:24, NLT). The selfish way is our distraction over trying to keep our glasses. It's the fretting and the pacing. It's the fear and the anxiety. It's the way of what's always been and not wanting to lose it. It's the realization of the cost of what's being lost (my life lived my way) and the inability to count it. It's idolatry.

I idolized my pair of glasses so much I spent almost two hours trying to fish them out of the river. I even broke my brand new fishing pole just trying one last-ditch effort to save the lost pair of glasses. In breaking the pole and losing time with my son, I more than doubled the cost in trying to get the glasses than they were actually worth. They weren't all that important to my life, and I am living just fine on this other side of their loss. So why the fixation? Why the idolization?

The endless attempts I made to get what I couldn't gain came out of selfishness. I didn't like the thought of buying a new pair of glasses. I resented the idea of having to take time during the week to go to the eye doctor to get an eye exam, to find a new pair of glasses, order them and then go back and get them fitted. I didn't like the thought of the interruption, so I put time with my son on hold while I tried to salvage the glasses so I could save my own time, money and week's schedule. I went away from our fishing trip full of regret. Regret is the way of selfishness. It's what we're left with on the other side of our self-centered ways.

~ ~ ~ ~ ~

We don't have to live with regret and loss. There is another way. It's called "relinquishment." Relinquishment is a lot like surrender. It's coming to Jesus with what I've been holding onto and letting my grip go slack. It's leaving the glasses in his hands and turning in a different direction. It's taking a new grip on a new reality—the cross. When we take up the cross, Jesus doesn't mean we are to enact carrying a massive wooden burden. What he's pointing us to is not the actual cross, but the life it represents. To take up the cross is to take up a new path in life, where we leave the glasses behind and instead draw near to Jesus. We become more and more cross-eyed as we let go of ourselves and our control over our lives; in doing so we give up our lives for Jesus' sake.

The result of this choice on the other side of our rescue is salvation and not resentment. "But if you give up your life for my sake, you will save it" (Matthew 16:25b, NLT). Where we could have lost everything we now gain everything through what we've been willing to lose. We've let go of what we could never gain and received what we can have: life with Jesus.

ON THE OTHER SIDE OF DAY 4:

Parable Principle: We don't have to live with regret and loss. There is another way. It's called "relinquishment."

Scripture Memory Verse for the Week: *"If you try to hang on to your life, you will lose it. But if you give up your life for my sake, you will save it" (Matthew 16:25, NLT).*

Questions for Reflection:

1. What are the lesser things you're distracted with in your life? Take time to name and define them.

2. If you're candid with your distraction(s), what do you know you're losing as a result of holding onto these things with a tight grip?

3. What would it take for you to let go of your "pair of glasses"?

4. How would your life be different if you turned from your selfish ways? What are some areas the Lord is calling you to be selfless in?

Taking a Quack at It:

Relinquishment requires a new focus. Take time today to turn from your selfish ways by exercising yourself in a different direction. E.g., if your tight-fisted with your wallet, spend sacrificially for the good of someone you know who is in need. If you're tight-lipped with words of love or affirmation, take time to speak your appreciation and care for someone who could benefit from those words.

Day 5: "Glasses in a Palm-Tree Stump"

> *1 Six days later Jesus took Peter and the two brothers, James and John, and led them up a high mountain to be alone. 2 As the men watched, Jesus' appearance was transformed so that his face shone like the sun, and his clothes became as white as light. 3 Suddenly, Moses and Elijah appeared and began talking with Jesus.*
>
> *4 Peter exclaimed, "Lord, it's wonderful for us to be here! If you want, I'll make three shelters as memorials—one for you, one for Moses, and one for Elijah."*
>
> *5 But even as he spoke, a bright cloud overshadowed them, and a voice from the cloud said, "This is my dearly loved Son, who brings me great joy. Listen to him."*

Like most families, we tend to keep things lit in our house at night. The kids each have a night light that pushes back the darkness when they head to bed. The hallway between their bedrooms stays bright during the nighttime hours. The kitchen has a lamp we keep glowing as well. All of these watts are used each and every night so that the Farrell family can see in the darkness.

I can remember my dislike for the dark starting way back as a small child. I distinctly recall a night when I was around five years old. My brother Matt and I snuck down from our upstairs bedroom into the kitchen to snatch some cookies. We had gotten the stash without waking anyone up, but once we realized we were all alone in a darkened kitchen, we both began to whimper and cry.

The same fear of the dark I experienced as a small boy came back to me with force at the river's edge. I knew my glasses were in the dark and hollowed-out palm tree stump, but I just couldn't go there. I could not, for the life of me, reach into the darkness to fish them out. I'm sure they were simply a few watery feet from my grasp; but without the ability to see in the darkness, there was no way I was gonna reach my hand into a cave-like recess. What's more, whatever's living in that space can now see in the dark. Maybe there is a four-eyed gator living in the Econ River and better able to snatch its next prey with 20/20 vision.

~ ~ ~ ~ ~

Jesus understands our fear of the dark. He knows how much we dislike not being able to see. That's why we find Jesus giving three of his disciples 20/20 vision in the dark of his coming suffering and death. Take a moment to read this portion of the biblical text again: "Six days later Jesus took Peter and the two brothers, James and John, and led them up a high mountain to be alone. As the men watched, Jesus' appearance was transformed so that his face shone like the sun, and his clothes became as white as light" (Matthew 17:1–2, NLT).

Peter, James and John did not like the feeling of heading into the dark reality of what Jesus had foretold. I'm sure the words of his rejection and death had filled their minds with questions and nightmares. They felt vulnerable, afraid, uneasy, alone. It could easily have become a place of paralysis or downright grounds to up and leave the path of discipleship. Maybe there was the sense of a bait and switch. Jesus was informing them of things they had not signed up for, and they weren't all too sure they wanted to continue following. I'm guessing they must have felt like I did looking into that dark palm tree stump. *There have to be river monsters waiting for me in there!* What's amazing is that Jesus doesn't poke fun or make light of their fears. Instead, Jesus turns a light on and brings them some comfort.

Take a moment to imagine what the disciples must have seen. There's Jesus, radiant! There are Moses and Elijah, famed men of old, with much courage and faith! The light must have been too much to take in. For a brief period of time the darkness the disciples have been cowering in is vaporized and undone. The three of them can see clearly and their fears are dispelled.

~ ~ ~ ~ ~

Rescued into a Life of Relinquishment

All of us can relate to Peter, James and John. Whether we're talking about the unexpected path of Jesus to the cross or the blindsiding experience of life throwing a curve, we've all encountered fear of the dark when it comes to following Jesus. We want to give up. We want to walk away. We're scared, angry, frightened, alone, weak and frail. Here's the truth: Jesus doesn't poke fun at us or make light of our fear. No, Jesus comes to us in the dark and he turns a light on. It may only last for a moment. Maybe an hour or short season is all that we have to see in the dark. The light may radiate briefly and then be snuffed out again. But no matter the length of time the light shines, our ability to see clearly in whatever darkness we're in is a sheer gift of welcome relief. We see, have seen, or will see at some point, and what we see will enable us to endure the night.

~ ~ ~ ~ ~

The result of seeing Jesus for who he is, is enlightening. "This is my dearly loved Son, who brings me great joy. Listen to him" (Matthew 17:5b, NLT). God gives us the gift to see in the dark not for the goal of seeing in the dark but for the ability to listen in the dark. Here's a life principle: **You may not be able to see in the dark, but you can always hear in the dark**. Do you hear Jesus in your darkness? He's speaking to you. He's calling your name. Jesus is the one who shepherds us in the valley of the shadow of death. The shadow may cast deep darkness over us, but the shepherd's voice can pierce any darkness. We follow Jesus as we listen to him. He leads us and we know his voice. It's a good and loving voice, able to instill courage and perseverance.

ON THE OTHER SIDE OF DAY 5:

Parable Principle: You may not be able to see in the dark, but you can always hear in the dark.

Scripture Memory Verse for the Week: *"If you try to hang on to your life, you will lose it. But if you give up your life for my sake, you will save it" (Matthew 16:25, NLT).*

Questions for Reflection:

1. Do you have a memory of a time you experienced a deep fear of the darkness? What happened?

2. Name a place of darkness in your life right now. Get detailed in your description of this area of darkness.

3. Where is the Lord in your darkness? Prayerfully consider this question.

4. What does the Lord want to reveal about himself in the midst of your darkness? How would this light affect you if you saw it and took it in?

5. What are some ways you can listen to Jesus' voice? Are there scriptures that bring comfort to you? If so, what are they and what do they say to you about Jesus' presence?

Taking a Quack at It:

Listening takes a lot of practice. It means persevering through the distractions and mental worries. Take 30 minutes to simply listen to Jesus. Don't say a word. Don't involve any of your own self-effort except listening. When distractions come to mind, keep on listening! Once done, reflect on the experience. What was it like?

Day 6: "Single Vision"

> 7 Then Jesus came over and touched them. "Get up," he said. "Don't be afraid." 8 And when they looked up, Moses and Elijah were gone, and they saw only Jesus.

Vision can be a funny thing. After I lost my glasses in the river I had to go back to my junk drawer at home and get out my old pair of glasses. Over the next several days my eyes strained to see; I got headaches and blurry vision. It was like I was seeing double sometimes. I wanted clarity of focus and no headaches. I wanted to go easy on my eyes and not have to strain. I wanted my eyes back.

Seeing double and having to strain the eyes is a hardship in the midst of daily living. Reading becomes a challenge, as does driving and watching TV. We were created to see with precision, and our heads hurt and our eyes wince until we do. Much the same is true of the disciples on the mountain. They see Jesus in all of his divine glory, but they also see Moses and Elijah. In fact, Peter was so enamored with the three of them that he wanted to make the place an extended-stay hotel. But Peter is reminded that there is only room for a single and precise vision when it comes to faith. "And when they looked up, Moses and Elijah were gone, and they saw only Jesus" (Matthew 17:8, NLT).

Aren't those beautiful words? "And they saw only Jesus." There is a place for Moses and Elijah. There's a place for people we look up to and admire. But **there is only one place for Jesus**. Jesus is far greater than any other. Infinitely so! In your life of faith, do you only see Jesus?

~ ~ ~ ~ ~

Lottie Strong lived up to her last name. Although she was in her 90s and lived alone in a doublewide, her ability to see only Jesus was inspiring to my new life of faith as a teenager. I'll never forget one afternoon when our youth pastor, Mark Brown, took us to see Lottie. I went expecting to visit an old woman who was feeble and frail. What I found was a vibrant person of faith who knew Jesus intimately well.

When we arrived at Lottie's house, she took us outside to her backyard. I assumed she had some lawn work or house maintenance she needed us to do. But she pointed at a well-worn path that went across the yard and into some nearby woods. Without batting an eye she picked up her cane and led us on a half-mile walk along the path. We were all confused. *Where's she taking us?* At the end of the walk we came to an open clearing that had a small mountain of rocks piled up. Lottie began to share with us that whenever she had a concern, anxiety or need, she'd carry a rock that represented her prayer request all the way from her house to this clearing and leave it in the hands of Jesus. Then she looked each of us in the eye and said that she had carried a rock on our behalf to this small mountain.

That mountain became, in some deeply meaningful way, my own mount of transfiguration. Seeing Lottie's faith changed me on the inside. I wanted her faith. I wanted to see Jesus and trust him as clearly as she did. In fact, Lottie became the very person who placed the call to preach on my life. She said that she prayed for me often while I pursued my pastoral education. I firmly believe that Lottie Strong is one of the primary reasons I'm in the ministry today.

~ ~ ~ ~ ~

Like Lottie Strong, we need to simply see Jesus sometimes. We need to bring to him our needs and concerns, and leave them in his hands. There's rest for you and me if we do so. What would it take to see only Jesus in your life? How would this singleness of vision remove your headaches? What would happen if you allowed your tired eyes to have some rest? "They saw only Jesus." Let that be your reality today and your refrain in the days to come.

ON THE OTHER SIDE OF DAY 6:

Parable Principle: There is only one place for Jesus.

Scripture Memory Verse for the Week: *"If you try to hang on to your life, you will lose it. But if you give up your life for my sake, you will save it" (Matthew 16:25, NLT).*

Questions for Reflection:

1. Are your eyes of faith strained? If so, why?

2. If you had to name where your focus tends to be, what would you come up with? What does this say about you?

3. What would it take to see only Jesus? What would have to happen in you to do so?

4. Are there some things that need to fade from your view? What are they and how are they hindering your life in Christ?

Taking a Quack at It:

Download the song or lyrics to "Be Thou My Vision." Meditate on the verses. Commit the song to memory and make it the prayer of your heart.

Day 7: Rest

Worship in community.

Enjoy the presence of loved ones.

Take time to take note of God's creation.

Reflect on this past week.

Commit this coming week to the Lord.

ENDNOTES

1   E. W. Blandy: *The United Methodist Hymnal*. Nashville, TN: The United Methodist Publishing House, 1989, #338.

2   Danny Morris, *Discerning God's Will Together: A Spiritual Practice for the Church*. Nashville, TN: Upper Room, 1997.

PARABLE 4

Bus 90:

Rescued into a Life of Courage

It was a hot afternoon in the beginning of September 1977. I was decked out in my bright plaid pants, thick white leather Sesame Street belt and my Mr. Snuffleupagus t-shirt. I was waiting for Bus 90 and was excited about my very first bus ride. My backpack was full and had that new plastic smell. My Walt Disney Thermos held a full day's serving of cold chocolate milk. Although I didn't know what to expect when the massive Thomas-built bus pulled up, I knew I was prepared.

I heard the bus before I saw it. It rounded a bend about a quarter of a mile down the street from where I stood on East River Road, and I could tell I was the next stop. I was relieved to see that it was bright yellow. I also liked the dim roar of the engine and the sound of the bus door when it opened. When I boarded the bus, I held onto the handrail with all of my might. I didn't want my first acquaintance with my peers to include me tripping and making a fool of myself. I arrived at the top of the steps without any trouble and met the bus driver, Ms. Nancy. At first sight she looked rather tired. She forced a smile, but I could see past the caked-on lipstick that the bus was the last place she wanted to be. She told me to quickly find a seat and to remain seated while the bus was in motion.

I remember looking down the aisle and wondering which of the countless green benches should become my seat. I didn't have a lot of time to make a choice, so I decided to sit in the front bench on the passenger side of the bus. I figured this spot would enable me to see out the massive front windows and allow me to keep an eye on how Ms. Nancy drove the bus.

The smell of diesel and the sound of the bus put me in a place of childhood wonder and joy. I was living every kindergartner's dream.

Although the ride was well over an hour, it was just what I had hoped it would be. It was scenic, loud and filled with the laughter and voices of my new friends. Looking back on that initial experience, I wish my first experience on Bus 90 had remained constant all throughout my years in the public school system. But the plain fact is that my kindergarten joy riding was cut short at the beginning of first grade. My arrival in first grade meant that I became a part of the larger school's daily schedule, and so the bus ride was filled not only with my Cookie-Monster-loving friends, but also all the other kids—from first grade up through high school.

When I began riding the bus with all the kids from all of the grades, I quickly learned there was an unspoken caste system at work on the bus. Kindergartners, first-, second- and third-graders were forced to sit in the front benches of the bus. There was usually a smattering of undesirable older kids who, through genetics or awkward social means, were also made to sit with us younger kids. But typically it was us little guys who had to endure the front of the bus. The purpose for us being in the front was not only because we were too young to get to enjoy the perks of the back benches where conversations could be raunchy and road bumps made you feel like you were on a rollercoaster, but because the backs of our heads made great targets for the older kids who were attempting to hone and strengthen their spit-wad capabilities.

In the center of the bus were the benches for the kids who found themselves in an uncertain and precarious social setting of acceptance and rejection. These kids were the early-blooming fourth- and fifth-graders, along with the junior high students. They were not on the level of the outcasts in the very front, nor were they fully accepted by the jocks and smokers in the back. They were the ones who were desperately trying to prove themselves to the back-benchers by way of torturing the front-benchers. Their success at poking fun or making a laughing stock of a nerd or a young child determined whether they would be sitting in the back benches the following school year. I feared this caste of kids the most when I was little. If you looked at one of them wrong when they got on the bus, you were guaranteed a whole lot of trouble. In the back of the bus were the jocks and the smokers. The jocks had the feathered hair and the Nike swooshes. The smokers wore the denim jackets and the khaki leather boots. Although these two groups didn't get along or run in the same social circles, they tended to share the back benches and hold utter control over whether or not the bus ride would be torturous or calm for the rest of us. In Mafioso style, they planned the hits on the little kids and decided, through rites of initiation, whether the middle-benchers had earned themselves a spot in the back of the bus.

As I reflect on my experience in that out-and-out habitat of social stigma and turbulence, I am amazed at the role of Ms. Nancy the bus driver. I don't know if she was paid off or had simply decided not to interfere with the caste system of the students, but there were unbelievable fights and dealings of all kinds going on during those bus rides that she never got in the middle of. I've come to the conclusion that she didn't have the courage to confront the back-benchers. She was afraid of them.

I knew this to be true all the way back in the first grade, when I boarded the bus one morning and was shocked to see two brand new stereo speakers on the left side of the bus's interior. The tape cassette was in and the volume was at full throttle. Although it was only 7:30 in the morning, the song of choice from the back-benchers was "Burn in Hell" by Judas Priest, and it blared across the vehicle with fury and heavy-metallic resonance. I remember the very first time I heard the song play; it sent chills down my 6-year-old spine and made my stomach churn. We didn't listen to that kind of music at home and the lyrics were not the kind my Sunday school teacher chopped out on the piano. Although I couldn't have named it at the time, I felt like I was losing something important on the inside. Innocence or a feeling of security was being taken from me. I looked around for someone to stop the music, but soon realized the person I would have normally turned to was the very person who had cranked the volume up.

Ms. Nancy had submitted to playing the music and didn't appear to mind its deafening nature. I was shocked. I couldn't believe that a woman the same age as my mom would allow that kind of music to be played on the bus. In that moment I can still recall how my regard for my bus driver hit an all-time low. Hellish music and hellish behavior created a living hell on Bus 90, and I had to endure it for the next nine years. How far we had fallen since my kindergarten year! Ms. Nancy had betrayed me.

~ ~ ~ ~ ~

My experience on Bus 90 is a lot like the cultural dynamics at work in our world today. If you're a Christian seeking to live the life of Jesus, you're in for trouble. There's no doubt about it. You see, trying to live a life of gratitude (week one), obedience (week two), and relinquishment (week three) in a culture that loves to listen to the lyrics of hellish social behaviors and standards is far from easy. Further, the local church often plays out the role of Ms. Nancy with perfection. A deaf ear and a blind eye is turned to unspeakable sin and brokenness, because the church lacks the courage to face the back-benchers of our culture.

If we are to be the church—the people of God who have been brought out of a shared rescue—we must be able to both understand and exhibit courage. Jesus said, "If the world hates you, remember that it hated me first. The world would love you as one of its own if you belonged to it, but you are no longer part of the world. I chose you to come out of the world, so it hates you. Do you remember what I told you? 'A slave is not greater than the master.' Since they persecuted me, naturally they will persecute you" (John 15:18–20a, NLT).

Hatred and animosity are not easy to shoulder. Being looked down upon or forced to the fringe of a society that is pursuing godless paths is not enjoyable. Nevertheless, Jesus calls us to live faithfully in the midst of hatred and persecution. The ability to be faithful requires a lot of courage, and this is why we'll be living in this virtue for the next six days.

BIBLICAL TEXT FOR WEEK 4: 1 PETER 3:8–4:19

[1 Peter 3] 8 Finally, all of you should be of one mind. Sympathize with each other. Love each other as brothers and sisters. Be tenderhearted, and keep a humble attitude. 9 Don't repay evil for evil. Don't retaliate with insults when people insult you. Instead, pay them back with a blessing. That is what God has called you to do, and he will bless you for it. 10 For the Scriptures say,

"If you want to enjoy life and see many happy days,
keep your tongue from speaking evil and your lips from telling lies.
11 Turn away from evil and do good.
Search for peace, and work to maintain it.
12 The eyes of the Lord watch over those who do right,

> and his ears are open to their prayers.
> But the Lord turns his face
> against those who do evil."

13 Now, who will want to harm you if you are eager to do good? 14 But even if you suffer for doing what is right, God will reward you for it. So don't worry or be afraid of their threats. 15 Instead, you must worship Christ as Lord of your life. And if someone asks about your Christian hope, always be ready to explain it. 16 But do this in a gentle and respectful way. Keep your conscience clear. Then if people speak against you, they will be ashamed when they see what a good life you live because you belong to Christ. 17 Remember, it is better to suffer for doing good, if that is what God wants, than to suffer for doing wrong!

18 Christ suffered for our sins once for all time. He never sinned, but he died for sinners to bring you safely home to God. He suffered physical death, but he was raised to life in the Spirit.

19 So he went and preached to the spirits in prison—20 those who disobeyed God long ago when God waited patiently while Noah was building his boat. Only eight people were saved from drowning in that terrible flood. 21 And that water is a picture of baptism, which now saves you, not by removing dirt from your body, but as a response to God from a clean conscience. It is effective because of the resurrection of Jesus Christ.

22 Now Christ has gone to heaven. He is seated in the place of honor next to God, and all the angels and authorities and powers accept his authority.

[1 Peter 4] 1 So then, since Christ suffered physical pain, you must arm yourselves with the same attitude he had, and be ready to suffer, too. For if you have suffered physically for Christ, you have finished with sin. 2 You won't spend the rest of your lives chasing your own desires, but you will be anxious to do the will of God. 3 You have had enough in the past of the evil things that godless people enjoy—their immorality and lust, their feasting and drunkenness and wild parties, and their terrible worship of idols.

4 Of course, your former friends are surprised when you no longer plunge into the flood of wild and destructive things they do. So they slan-

der you. 5 But remember that they will have to face God, who will judge everyone, both the living and the dead. 6 That is why the Good News was preached to those who are now dead—so although they were destined to die like all people, they now live forever with God in the Spirit.

7 The end of the world is coming soon. Therefore, be earnest and disciplined in your prayers. 8 Most important of all, continue to show deep love for each other, for love covers a multitude of sins. 9 Cheerfully share your home with those who need a meal or a place to stay.

10 God has given each of you a gift from his great variety of spiritual gifts. Use them well to serve one another. 11 Do you have the gift of speaking? Then speak as though God himself were speaking through you. Do you have the gift of helping others? Do it with all the strength and energy that God supplies. Then everything you do will bring glory to God through Jesus Christ. All glory and power to him forever and ever! Amen.

12 Dear friends, don't be surprised at the fiery trials you are going through, as if something strange were happening to you. 13 Instead, be very glad—for these trials make you partners with Christ in his suffering, so that you will have the wonderful joy of seeing his glory when it is revealed to all the world.

14 So be happy when you are insulted for being a Christian, for then the glorious Spirit of God[m] rests upon you. 15 If you suffer, however, it must not be for murder, stealing, making trouble, or prying into other people's affairs. 16 But it is no shame to suffer for being a Christian. Praise God for the privilege of being called by his name! 17 For the time has come for judgment, and it must begin with God's household. And if judgment begins with us, what terrible fate awaits those who have never obeyed God's Good News? 18 And also,

"If the righteous are barely saved,
    what will happen to godless sinners?"

19 So if you are suffering in a manner that pleases God, keep on doing what is right, and trust your lives to the God who created you, for he will never fail you.

Day 1: "Courage to Refrain"

> 8 Finally, all of you should be of one mind. Sympathize with each other. Love each other as brothers and sisters. Be tenderhearted, and keep a humble attitude. 9 Don't repay evil for evil. Don't retaliate with insults when people insult you. Instead, pay them back with a blessing. That is what God has called you to do, and he will bless you for it. 10 For the Scriptures say,
>
> "If you want to enjoy life
>   and see many happy days,
> keep your tongue from speaking evil
>   and your lips from telling lies.
> 11 Turn away from evil and do good.
>   Search for peace, and work to maintain it.
> 12 The eyes of the Lord watch over those who do right,
>   and his ears are open to their prayers.
> But the Lord turns his face
>   against those who do evil."

The biblical text for this week comes out of 1 Peter. I chose this text because it's believed that Peter's letter was delivered to scattered Christians over the northern part of modern Turkey. The timing of the letter places it close to the outbreak of the Neronian persecution in A.D. 64. This was a time when believers suffered dearly for their faith in Jesus. In fact, suffering is a primary theme in this letter, and so it made sense to utilize a portion of this text to address the need for courage.

Often the concept of courage is thought to have arisen out of the lives and stories of the great Greek warriors such as Achilles. Given this background, it's easy to see how courage could be associated with physical prowess, mental boldness or the capacity to have a manly manner. In fact, the Greek word for courage is *arête*, which is sometimes associated with the name of Ares, the Greek god of war, and *andreia*, the Greek word for "male." So these Greek origins for the word "courage" conjure up images of battle-hardened soldiers. However, the word "courage" in the Bible conveys a much different image. The Hebrew word *hazaq* means to "show oneself strong." Other words like *ruah* (literally, "spirit"), *lebab* (the Hebrew word for "heart") and *amas* (to "be quick or alert"), exhibit the basic kind of attitude from which courage flows.[1]

The early Church studied the virtue of courage in great detail. Later, Thomas Aquinas, one of the greatest thinkers of the Medieval Age, put a definition to this virtue that best encapsulates what followers of Jesus have learned about this inner posture of fortitude:

> [C]ourage is chiefly concerned with fears of difficulties likely to cause the will to retreat from following the lead of reason. But courage ought not merely to endure unflinchingly the pressure of difficult situations by restraining fear; it ought also to make a calculated attack, when it is necessary to eliminate difficulties in order to win safety for the future. Such action appears to be daring. Therefore courage is concerned with fears and acts of daring, restraining the first and measuring the second.[2]

Notice how Aquinas incorporates postures of resistance and of attack, as well as the central role of reason. Taking Aquinas' lead, we can conclude that the virtue of courage is multifaceted. It has a lot of nuances to it that we can seek to understand and purposefully engage in. One of these, the topic for this day, is the courage to refrain.

~ ~ ~ ~

Rusty's hair matched his name. Freckle-faced and small in stature, he didn't look all that imposing but he was as fierce as the countless Dobermans guarding his family's metal scrap heaps that surrounded their unkempt house. He lived no more than three miles up the "big hill" from where we got picked up by the school bus. I was always curious about Rusty and his family. I had never caught sight of his mom or his dad, but I had spotted his older brothers in the scrap heaps when our bus passed their house. They had a crazy look in their eyes like Lew Zealand, the boomerang fish thrower on *The Muppet Show*. They made you scared just by looking at you.

Maybe it was because he was so small in size that he was so mean. Perhaps he'd gotten knocked around at home by his brothers or his dad; or maybe just living in a shack most kids gawked at and made fun of put Rusty in a bad relational place. I was never sure what created the mean streak in Rusty, but I didn't want to be in his path.

One morning Rusty entered the bus and I could smell a fight brewing.

Who's gonna get clobbered? I sort of watched Rusty walk down the aisle, but at the same time pretended not to. I didn't want to issue an unspoken invitation. Rusty's small beady eyes were roaming the front benches looking for a target. He found one in poor Mikey.

"Hey, fatso!" Rusty shouted.

Mikey pretended not to hear or take the comment on his husky build too personally.

"Hey, Mikey! Yeah, you! Hey, fatso, you wanna get punched?"

Rusty was in rare form. It'd been a couple of weeks since he'd last tasted blood, and he was hungry. Mikey kept looking out the window. Adrenaline was coursing through Rusty's veins and his face turned a radish shade of red. As usual, Ms. Nancy pretended not to take notice. Mikey was dead meat.

Although the bus was in motion, Rusty stood firmly planted in the aisle, staring at Mikey and hoping that Mikey would give him one good reason to make his fists sore. A muffled chant began to grow.

"Do it! Do it! Do it! Do it," the back-benchers called.

In one last-ditch effort to give the onlookers an answer to their mantra, Rusty said, "Hey, fatty! You chicken?"

Now we all know those are fighting words, but were they worth the fight for Mikey? I watched and wondered what would happen next. Unfortunately, Mikey must have sized up the incredibly pitiful kid who got his kicks hurting younger kids and decided it was worth the fight. So he spoke back. Rusty gave him the clock-cleaning of a lifetime. Rusty must have thrown a hundred punches, and it looked like every one of them landed on poor Mikey's face. After the incendiary attack, Rusty walked to the back of the bus and sat down with the back-benchers, showing off a broad and proud smile. I felt awful for Mikey, but I found myself feeling even worse for Rusty. Mikey could get over the lickin' he got that morning, but Rusty would probably live the highest moments of his life on Bus 90 and be stuck in a metal scrap heap the rest of it. For him, this opportunity to treat an innocent kid with a whole lot of evil was a bright spot in what must have been a pretty nightmarish existence.

~ ~ ~ ~ ~

Mikey's experience with Rusty on Bus 90 taught me the value of refraining from action. Rusty baited Mikey with a whole lot of fightin' words and unfortunately Mikey paid back evil with evil. The result was brokenness for the both of them. If Mikey had restrained his tongue, the fist pounding wouldn't have started. Rusty's satisfaction in conquering one more innocent kid wouldn't have been satiated.

Whether we're on Bus 90 or in a stretch limo, there will always be Rustys in your life and my life. Sometimes restraint is the most courageous thing we can do in response to their evil actions and words. There will be times in your life and my life when we might be taunted, made fun of, or prompted to enter into a ring where fighting only makes the personal pain and brokenness of the other person all the more pronounced. On those occasions we've got to be willing to ask ourselves: **Is this worth the fight? Sometimes the godliest answer to that question is "No," and we need to have the courage to refrain.**

~ ~ ~ ~ ~

Peter knew all about courage. He had witnessed Jesus' suffering and death at the hands of vicious men. Even the bus driver at the time, Pilate, did nothing to stop the abuse. Although Jesus had done nothing to deserve the inhumane pummeling he received, the Bible says he endured it with a unique kind of courage. "He was led like a sheep to the slaughter. And as a lamb is silent before the shearers, he did not open his mouth. He was humiliated and received no justice" (Acts 8:32b–33a, NLT). Jesus could have wiped out his persecutors with a single blow, but he chose not to. Jesus could have utterly defeated the instigators of his beatings and death on the cross, but he did not fight back. He refrained, and through his weakness the power of Easter became a reality.

I think Peter's witness of Jesus' trial, suffering and death is what's behind the text for today. Peter instructs, "Don't repay evil for evil. Don't retaliate with insults when people insult you. Instead, pay them back with a blessing. That is what God has called you to do, and he will bless you for it" (I Peter 3:9, NLT). Peter is reminding us to respond to our Rustys with the same posture Jesus had.

Peter's counsel is necessary in our lives because we tend to want to give punch for punch and insult for insult. But this is not the courage Jesus exhibited when he was being insulted and persecuted. Oddly enough,

Jesus paid all of his Rustys back with a blessing. He said from the cross, "Father, forgive them, for they don't know what they are doing" (Luke 23:34, NLT). Take a moment to think on what Jesus asked his Father for. Jesus isn't just saying something that sounds nice to the mocking "Do it! Do it! Do it!" attitudes of the crowd. Jesus is literally asking his Father to bless the very people who have nailed him to the cross. Where there is insult, injury, abuse, mocking laughter and merciless treatment, Jesus responds with courageous restraint and goes even further by paying them all back with a blessing of forgiveness. Jesus models for us the courage of restraint.

What if Jesus had retaliated? Would Easter morning have happened? Would new life out of death and the power of forgiveness become available to us? Absolutely not! But still it's hard for us to wrap ourselves around the concept of courage as restraint. We're too much like Peter used to be. Remember when Peter was with Jesus in the Garden of Gethsemane? The betrayer had come for Jesus, along with a whole entourage of back-benchers. In response, Peter took action and cut off the ear of the high priest's slave. Jesus was outraged. "Put away your sword," Jesus told him. "Those who use the sword will die by the sword. Don't you realize that I could ask my Father for thousands of angels to protect us, and he would send them instantly? But if I did, how would the Scriptures be fulfilled that describe what must happen now?" (Matthew 26:52–54, NLT).

What Jesus is saying is that sometimes the Father's purpose is fulfilled through restraint. This is a passive posture that honors God. Now you may find this whole approach to courage to be uncomfortable. Like Peter, maybe you lean toward action and lashing out in anger when you feel threatened. But notice what Peter learned and underscores in our text for today: "Turn away from evil and do good. Search for peace, and work to maintain it. The eyes of the Lord watch over those who do right, and his ears are open to their prayers. But the Lord turns his face against those who do evil" (I Peter 3:11–12, NLT).

The Father was watching over Jesus when he was betrayed in the Garden of Gethsemane. Like Jesus said, he could have asked for angelic protection and the Father would have instantly responded. So Jesus' restraint didn't reflect a lack of faith in his Father's presence; rather, he refrained from retaliation in full awareness that his Father was fully present to him. I'd even go so far as to say that the knowledge of his Father's presence was the reason Jesus was able to refrain from paying back evil with evil. Jesus was working for peace through his suffering and death, and he was confident that at the end of the day the Rustys of his reality would not win the fight. Ironically enough, the Father would turn his face against those who do evil but would give all attention to those who do good.

On the Other Side of Day 1:

Parable Principle: Is this worth the fight? Sometimes the godliest answer to that question is "No," and we need to have the courage to refrain.

Scripture Memory Verse for the Week: *"If you are suffering in a manner that pleases God, keep on doing what is right, and trust your lives to the God who created you, for he will never fail you"* (I Peter 4:19, NLT).

Questions for Reflection:

1. What's the most memorable act of courage you have witnessed in your life? Why has it stuck with you?

2. How would you define "courage"? Why?

3. Sometimes courage is the decision to refrain from action. Name an example of this kind of courage (e.g., Ghandi and non-violence in India).

4. What did Jesus mean when he said, "Those who use the sword die by the sword"? Do you agree?

5. What strikes you about Jesus' prayer of blessing from the cross?

6. What would it mean for you to repay evil with good in your present relationships and circumstances?

Taking a Quack at It:

Take some time to name those who are insulting you or paying you evil in your life right now. Ask the Lord what it would look like to repay those same people with a blessing. Remember, boundaries are important, so repaying with a blessing doesn't necessarily mean being in close contact or relationship with the Rustys in your life. Rather, we can repay with a blessing from a safe distance if we need to.

Day 2: "Courage to do Good"

> 13 Now, who will want to harm you if you are eager to do good? 14 But even if you suffer for doing what is right, God will reward you for it. So don't worry or be afraid of their threats. 15 Instead, you must worship Christ as Lord of your life. And if someone asks about your Christian hope, always be ready to explain it. 16 But do this in a gentle and respectful way. Keep your conscience clear. Then if people speak against you, they will be ashamed when they see what a good life you live because you belong to Christ. 17 Remember, it is better to suffer for doing good, if that is what God wants, than to suffer for doing wrong!

Bus 90 was the very first place I ever shared my faith in Jesus openly. I remember like it was yesterday, sitting in my bench on the bus. I had just read out of my cartoon Bible the night before of how Jesus would come and gather all people together for the Judgment Day. He would separate all of us like goats from sheep. The former had a painful eternal reality to face and the latter had a deeply good one to experience. The scripture was troubling to me, and so when Judas Priest's song, "Burn in Hell," had ended and my third grade peers were jeering and laughing about the song and the lyrics, I found myself feeling like I needed to tell them about heaven.

My friends noticed that I didn't join in with their approval of the song, and so they began to ask me why I didn't like the music the back-benchers were playing. I abruptly told them that Jesus was coming back someday. They looked at me as though I was out of my mind. Where's this kid coming from? I then proceeded to inform them that if we didn't believe in Jesus and follow him we could very well experience what Judas Priest had sung about (this is the evangelism-off-of-heavy-metal approach). They began to snicker at me. I remember feeling my face turn hot and beads of sweat forming on my forehead. I felt stupid. I regretted having shared about Jesus, and I recall lacking the ability to put words to what

I really wanted to say. I was tongue-tied, and what I said and the way I said it had come off different than I had intended.

Sharing Jesus with my friends on Bus 90 lasted five minutes. I don't know if it ever affected them in a positive way. I think they probably thought I was a little out there and began to distance themselves from me. I never approached the topic again during that school year, and for several days after the event I tried my best to recover. Fortunately summer break was nearing and I could hide out in the offseason. I desperately wanted to fade from view.

~ ~ ~ ~ ~

Communicating our faith in Jesus can be difficult because we all fear the experience I had on Bus 90. We don't like the idea of getting into a conversation where we'll get tongue tied and as a result lose the friends we have. We'd just as soon fade from view and hide out. Yet Peter says, "If someone asks about your Christian hope, always be ready to explain it. But do this in a gentle and respectful way. Keep your conscience clear" (I Peter 3:15). What Peter is calling us to on the other side of our rescue is the willingness to courageously share our hope in Jesus. Let's take a closer look.

Peter starts off by saying, "If someone asks about your Christian hope." In order for someone to ask about our Christian hope, they need to know that we have a hope in the first place. This is not a guessing game we play with the people who know us. This is not a minor hope on our part that for some strange reason the people who know us will ask about our faith in Jesus. Rather, a person only asks for more details when we've already been open enough to express what we believe. In the language of courage, this is called taking the offensive.

Offensive courage gives a follower of Christ more options when it comes to timing, how what's going to be shared will be shared, and the context where the sharing will best take place. Courage of resistance (cf. day one of this week) is a different form of courage in the sense that offensive courage takes a real mustering of the will and guts to initiate the communication of the gospel. It involves taking a risk. You might lose friends or the respect of those around you when they learn that you're a follower of Jesus. Simply put, taking an offensive posture means the burden of losing respect or relationships is on the person taking the initiative.

Most Christians refrain from sharing their faith so they don't have to feel responsible for the demise of a relationship. We like the feelings of being accepted, and so choosing to live nonverbally is easier than a face-to-face discussion where your feet are firmly planted in Jesus no matter what the other person might think.

Yet Peter presses the issue further, stating, "If someone asks about your Christian hope, always be ready to explain it" (I Peter 3:15, NLT). The readiness to explain one's Christian hope is another way of saying that we are to have an offensive posture. This is where I failed miserably on Bus 90. I knew I wanted to share my faith, but I wasn't prepared to share it. It came out horribly wrong, and the odd looks and reactions were probably due to how unprepared I was. If I had been prepared, I could have simply said what I felt needed saying in the way that most made sense.

We need to be ready to explain our hope. What we want to say and how we want to say it can be prepared in advance. The examples that matter most to us. The experiences that have had the deepest impact. The points that best communicate why we've come into our rescue and why we choose to hold onto our joyful hope in Jesus need to be as near to our tongues as they are to our minds and hearts. Peter calls us to be ready. This is taking the offensive and requires a lot of courage.

Peter also makes a point to describe how we are to share our faith. "And if someone asks about your Christian hope, always be ready to explain it. But do this in a gentle and respectful way. Keep your conscience clear" (I Peter 3:15–16, NLT). When we share our faith, particularly with those who may look at us with mock disbelief or condescension, we have to get clear on the fact that how we share it is as important as what we share. It's easy to reply angrily to those who distance themselves from our convictions, but Peter cautions us to use gentleness and respect.

The roles of gentleness and respect are critical today because it takes much more relational effort to evangelize people. The old Roman Road may still be a path, but it's a more difficult one to use to get from the Point A of a person's interest to the Point B of that same person's acceptance-of-Jesus' rescue. Relationship, gentleness and respect are the need of today if we are to share our hope in a way that honors the other person and draws them into a life of faith. Sharing in a manner that is gentle and respectful requires more courage as it's quite easy to lash out at those who may look down upon the hope we share. Yet as we persevere in intentionally giving respect, the ultimate results will be far better than if we didn't.

Our text for the day reminds us that we are not only to courageously share our hope, we are also to live it out. Notice that the sharing comes first and then how we live our lives after the verbalization of our hope comes second. Peter says, "If people speak against you, they will be ashamed when they see what a good life you live because you belong to Christ. Remember, it is better to suffer for doing good, if that is what God wants, than to suffer for doing wrong!" (I Peter 3:16b–17, NLT).

Peter is pointing out that people may very well speak against what we say we believe, but they will have a real hard time arguing against how we live our lives. The courage to live a godly life (the focus for week 6) takes intentional discipline. Praying for those who may persecute us, refraining from paying back evil for evil, and blessing those who insult us are all ways in which we can lead a good life in front of those who speak against our hope and faith.

~ ~ ~ ~ ~

E. Stanley Jones is more than likely the most revered and well known evangelist of the 20th century. There's not another person (save Billy Graham) who had a larger global impact when it came to sharing the hope of Jesus Christ through the spoken word. Jones was a courageous speaker who took the initiative to thoroughly consider what he would preach, the context he would speak in, and the manner in which the message would be given. His willingness to reach out with gentleness and respect to unbelieving skeptics, particularly in the countries of India and Japan, reflected his courage to both speak and act in a way that honored people of other cultures.

What I admire most about E. Stanley Jones was not just the message he gave, but the kind of life he lived. He was a follower of Jesus who had the courage to do good. He purposefully chose to guard his hope in Jesus with the kinds of morals and ethics no one could fault. E. Stanley Jones was never at the center of a scandal or inappropriate ethical decision. He made sure to back his verbal message with a godly life. A lot of Christians today have come to believe that we are unable to live a godly life. The Church is assumed to be a place of hypocrites and that's

Rescued into a Life of Courage

all we can possibly hope for. Holiness of heart and life and high ethical standards are scoffed at. Yet Jones always approached the courage of his convictions in Jesus with an understanding that his ability to courageously share his faith and live a life of godliness was not by his own power but through Jesus. Jones says, "'Able for anything'—my motto. I repeat it to myself again and again and again. And I repeat it as the years come and go: 'I am able for anything'—anything he calls me to do. For his calls are his enablements. 'Without him, not one step over the threshold; with him, anywhere.'"[3] Offensive courage out of the enablements of the Lord; we would do well to open ourselves to sharing and living the hope of Jesus the way E. Stanley Jones once did.

~ ~ ~ ~ ~

The local church is called to live into an offensive kind of courage. We need to be willing to verbalize the hope we have in Jesus, even if it means relational risk. We also need to share in a way that is intentional, gentle and respectful. Further, the way we live gives credibility to what we say our hope is in. If we speak with our lips one thing and live our lives as though we believe something totally different, we lose the ability to draw people to Jesus. You see, people may cause us to feel red in the face if they don't understand or accept what we believe, but if we persevere and live good and godly lives, those who reject our message may wind up accepting it in the long run as they can't argue with the way we choose to live.

~ ~ ~ ~ ~

One of my friends, whom I often passed while riding Bus 90, journeyed through all of the school grades with me. We grew up together, though eventually we began to walk in different directions. When we first met we shared the same hope in Jesus. In fact, he was planning to go into the ministry. I looked up to his love for Jesus. I respected his desire to become a pastor. He challenged me in my life of faith.

Over time I grew increasingly involved at a really vibrant local church while my friend began to break away from his local church. Karate became his passion, as did body building. Our social circles also began to differ. His friends became more of the party crowd, and mine were more and more the teens who attended church with me. By the end of high school we were completely different breeds of people. We didn't talk as much and we didn't share much in common. But I'll never forget one of the last weeks of our senior year when he looked at me and said, "Tim, I just want to tell you that I've watched you over the years. It might sound funny to you, but I've never heard you say one curse word. I really respect that and I just want you to know that I look up to you."

I was shocked! I had no idea the kind of influence the Lord was having on my friend through my lack of participating in the cursing and filthy language of our peers. Although we didn't share the same hope anymore, he saw in the way I chose to live something to admire. It's reminded me ever since of the value of Peter's words, "Keep your conscience clear. Then if people speak against you, they will be ashamed when they see what a good life you live because you belong to Christ" (I Peter 3:16b).

ON THE OTHER SIDE OF DAY 2:

Parable Principle: Most Christians refrain from sharing their faith so they don't have to feel responsible for the demise of a relationship.

Scripture Memory Verse for the Week: *"If you are suffering in a manner that pleases God, keep on doing what is right, and trust your lives to the God who created you, for he will never fail you" (I Peter 4:19, NLT).*

Question for Reflection:

1. Have you ever been asked about your Christian hope? If so, what was the experience like?

2. Have you lost a friendship because you shared your faith?

3. Have you ever thought out what you'd want to share with others about your relationship with Jesus? What are the main experiences and truths that would be most important for you to communicate?

4. Have you ever seen a person share their Christian convictions in an angry and disrespectful way? How did that impact the person(s) on the receiving end?

5. What degree of importance do you place on living a good life because you belong to Christ? How would you describe the kind of life you actually live? Does your life support your Christian hope?

Rescued into a Life of Courage

Taking a Quack at It:

Take some time to create an outline of your personal relationship with Jesus. How have you experienced his rescue, and what are the main things you'd want others to know about your story? Jot down the main concepts and rehearse it with a friend or family member. Get to a place where what you'd want to share makes sense, and then begin to pray for opportunities to share.

Day 3: "Courage with a Purpose"

> *18 Christ suffered for our sins once for all time. He never sinned, but he died for sinners to bring you safely home to God. He suffered physical death, but he was raised to life in the Spirit.*
>
> *19 So he went and preached to the spirits in prison—20 those who disobeyed God long ago when God waited patiently while Noah was building his boat. Only eight people were saved from drowning in that terrible flood. 21 And that water is a picture of baptism, which now saves you, not by removing dirt from your body, but as a response to God from a clean conscience. It is effective because of the resurrection of Jesus Christ.*
>
> *22 Now Christ has gone to heaven. He is seated in the place of honor next to God, and all the angels and authorities and powers accept his authority.*

It had been a long day at school, and I just wanted the bus ride to be over with. We were thirty minutes in and there were at least thirty more to go, when the flicking started up. I had been sitting by the window trying to fall asleep, when I felt the pain in my right ear. I immediately turned my head to see what had caused the hurt. Nothing. Must be dreaming. I went back to nodding off when something hit my right ear again. This time I heard someone begin to laugh in the bench behind me. I instantly knew I had become a target of the back-benchers. Playing it cool, I pretended nothing had happened. *Flick!* My ear had been hit again. More laughter. I began to get angry. *What's with the flicking?*

I decided to take the hand-swatter approach to stop whoever it was that was flicking my ear. But the hand movement through the small space between the side of the bench and the metal frame of bus window was way too fast. Before I knew it I had been flicked again. My right ear began to tingle and turn numb. The laughter from the benches behind me increased. So I went back to ignoring the flicking hand with the hopes that whoever was doing it would get bored and stop. *Flick. Flick. Flick. Flick. Flick. Flick.* It continued with renewed energy.

As fifteen or so minutes passed, my ear must have turned a bright tomato red. Although I had believed the behavior to be completely stupid, I had gone on ignoring it—thinking I could just forget it and never give the back-benchers the satisfaction of seeing me get upset. But my ear really started to hurt. The thought of the uninvited torture that was coming my way made me angrier and angrier and angrier. Somewhere before the fiftieth flick I decided to follow the lead of my anger and— sure enough, when the hand came in for the strike I grabbed the wrist as hard as I could and stood straight up. I don't think Chris knew what to do with me. I had always been pegged as a front-bench loser and standing up to the back-benchers was never a consideration in his mind. He had assumed I'd just take the flicking 'til I got home. But there I was, hurting his wrist and looking into his eyes with a William the Conqueror kind of death stare. "Stop flicking my ear!" I said. Chris stared back at me with dinner-plate-sized eyes.

When I let go of his wrist and sat back down, I never received another flick. I had demanded a full surrender and Chris was in full retreat. For one of the very first times I felt a surge of strength and pride course through my veins. I couldn't believe I had stood up for myself, and all the other front-benchers for that matter, and defied the bullies.

~ ~ ~ ~ ~

Early conceptions of courage always included the role of reason. It was believed that for courage to be a true virtue, there must be rational thought behind it; otherwise it was simply rash behavior or a mindless reaction. Putting this in today's lingo, I'd say that **courageous behavior needs to have a rational purpose in mind**.

When I stood up with courage to confront Chris who was flicking my ear, there was a purpose in my mind. The first purpose was to get the flicking to stop and salvage my wounded lobe. The second and greater purpose was to stand up for all of us front-benchers. In *Braveheart's* William-Wallace language, I was attempting to cry, "Freedom!" I guess you could say this was my own elementary version of the Battle of Sterling.

~ ~ ~ ~ ~

The Bible tells us that Jesus' courageous act of suffering and going to his death on a cross had a lot of reason and purpose behind it. I don't think Jesus woke up one morning and mindlessly pursued a course that would get him crucified. Rather, much of Jesus' public ministry was taken up with thinking through and purposefully setting his face toward Jerusalem (cf. Matthew 16:21–26; Matthew 17:22; Luke 9:51; Luke 22:39–46). Jesus' courage was virtuous because it pursued a purposeful end. Peter says, "Christ suffered for our sins once for all time. He never sinned, but he died for sinners to bring you safely home to God" (I Peter 3:18, NLT). Peter is saying that Jesus' courage to suffer and die was for the purpose of bringing us front-bench rejects safely home to God. Jesus didn't deserve the flicking. Jesus was sinless. But he took the suffering and the cross so that we who are the guilty ones can come home to the God who loves us.

Further, Peter points out that, "(Jesus) went and preached to the spirits in prison—those who disobeyed God long ago when God waited patiently while Noah was building his boat. Only eight people were saved from drowning in that terrible flood" (I Peter 3:19–20, NLT). I love these two verses that have undergone a lot of debate throughout the years. John Wesley believed that the preaching Jesus did occurred during the days of Noah, when this ark builder tried to warn the people of the destruction that was coming their way. Other scholars say that Jesus actually went to the spirits of those who had disobeyed God long ago for the purpose of preaching (literally, heralding) his victory. I like the way Eugene Peterson puts it in *The Message* because it seems to tie into what Peter says a little later in chapter four, verse six: "He went and proclaimed God's salvation to earlier generations who ended up in the prison of judgment because they wouldn't listen" (I Peter 3:19, THE MESSAGE).[4]

You see, Jesus not only had a purposeful courage that cried "Freedom!" on behalf of all forgotten and sinful front-benchers; he also journeyed down the center aisle and reached out to the disobedient back-benchers. Through Jesus' courage, both the flickee and the flicker get to get in on the purposeful suffering and death of Jesus that can bring all of us safely home to God. That's amazingly good news that we never have to get bored of.

~ ~ ~ ~

The Church can take a big lesson from Jesus' courage. Rather than be reactionary in this world—or ignore the people around us that tend to turn our ears red—we need to start purposefully praying and talking together about how we can proclaim freedom through Jesus to every front, middle and back-bencher. The steps we take as local churches need to have rational thought and prayerful purpose. We would do well to put down our *Robert's Rules of Order*, where majority votes win, and take up a courageous and open posture with Jesus in the Garden of Gethsemane, where we wrestle and pray over the gut-wrenching plans and purposes God has for us. Here's the thing: As we follow our suffering Lord, we'll know as he did what it feels like to experience victory in a world that enjoys flicking one another's ears.

ON THE OTHER SIDE OF DAY 3:

Parable Principle: Courageous behavior needs to have a rational purpose in mind.

Scripture Memory Verse for the Week: *"If you are suffering in a manner that pleases God, keep on doing what is right, and trust your lives to the God who created you, for he will never fail you" (I Peter 4:19, NLT).*

Questions for Reflection:

1. Have you ever had your ear flicked? Recount that experience of being bullied. What was it like?

2. Have you ever flicked someone's ear? Why'd you do it?

3. Do you agree that, for courage to be a virtue, it requires reason? Why or why not?

4. How does Jesus' purpose for courageously suffering and dying impact you?

5. What do you make of the whole "preaching to the people of Noah's day" portion of today's scripture?

6. How is the Lord calling you to move into purposeful courage?

Taking a Quack at It:

Jesus intentionally set his face toward Jerusalem. He journeyed there for a purpose. Although none of us carries the weight of Jesus' purpose, what is your Jerusalem? Take some time to begin to wrestle with what God is calling you to be about in your life, relationships, vocation, etc.

Day 4: "Courage to Persevere"

> *1 So then, since Christ suffered physical pain, you must arm yourselves with the same attitude he had, and be ready to suffer, too. For if you have suffered physically for Christ, you have finished with sin. 2 You won't spend the rest of your lives chasing your own desires, but you will be anxious to do the will of God. 3 You have had enough in the past of the evil things that godless people enjoy—their immorality and lust, their feasting and drunkenness and wild parties, and their terrible worship of idols.*
>
> *4 Of course, your former friends are surprised when you no longer plunge into the flood of wild and destructive things they do. So they slander you. 5 But remember that they will have to face God, who will judge everyone, both the living and the dead. 6 That is why the Good News was preached to those who are now dead—so although they were destined to die like all people, they now live forever with God in the Spirit.*
>
> *7 The end of the world is coming soon. Therefore, be earnest and disciplined in your prayers. 8 Most important of all, continue to show deep love for each other, for love covers a multitude of sins. 9 Cheerfully share your home with those who need a meal or a place to stay.*
>
> *10 God has given each of you a gift from his great variety of spiritual gifts. Use them well to serve one another. 11 Do you have the gift of speaking? Then speak as though God himself were speaking*

through you. Do you have the gift of helping others? Do it with all the strength and energy that God supplies. Then everything you do will bring glory to God through Jesus Christ. All glory and power to him forever and ever! Amen.

Bus 90 was a reality I persevered in. There were countless boring rides. There were trips in the winter when we'd get stuck on the "big hill" and have to wait what seemed like hours for help. There were the bus rides that came on the heels of school letting out for the summer (those were the best), and there were the times that the weather was at its peak of beauty and all the windows were open so the crisp autumn air diluted the smell of the noxious diesel. There were good times on the bus and horribly awful moments. In all of it, I simply persevered.

I persevered on Bus 90 because of one single reality: the future. I knew that I would not always ride that bus and, when I graduated from high school, the caste system, the abrasive music, the indifference of Ms. Nancy... all of it would be a thing of the past. There would come a day when I would drive my own car and follow my own route without getting my ear flicked. I had a certain hope.

~ ~ ~ ~ ~

Courage and perseverance are first-cousins. They go together. To persevere requires courage. To be courageous means you're gonna have to persevere. But in order to persevere there has to be a future hope in mind. Peter points this out when he says, "You have had enough in the past of the evil things that godless people enjoy—their immorality and lust, their feasting and drunkenness and wild parties, and their terrible worship of idols. Of course, your former friends are surprised when you no longer plunge into the flood of wild and destructive things they do. So they slander you. But remember that they will have to face God, who will judge everyone, both the living and the dead" (I Peter 4:3–5, NLT).

In these verses, Peter is reminding the recipients of his letter that there is a future reality that is coming their way. Like the looming flood that Noah spoke of in his day, so too there is a rising sense with each passing moment that one day we will all stand before God and be judged. It's in light of this future hope and certain day of the Lord that we are to live.

This future reality gives the people Peter is communicating with a handle to hold onto. They may be facing physical suffering (such as Neronian persecution, mentioned earlier) or they may have to stomach relational suffering in the form of slander (cf. 4:4); but they can be certain they will be able to persevere as long as they remember that one day we will all have to face God, who will right wrongs, restore those who have suffered, those who have been forgotten and those who have been slandered.

~ ~ ~ ~ ~

The Church needs Peter's reminder today because we live in-between competing realities. One reality says that what people think about us is all that matters. Their judgment and the fear of their slander is what we need to avoid. But the other reality is what Peter brings to the fore. He warns us to remember what's coming. We'll all have to face God, and what he thinks and how he judges our hearts is what will matter the most in that future day. So live in light of this greater concern; i.e., learn to take in the slander of those who don't understand your godly life, because you won't be able to stomach God's judgment if you fail to persevere.

Eugene Peterson, the author behind *The Message*, has a book called *A Long Obedience in the Same Direction*. This book journeys through the Songs of Ascent in the Old Testament's Book of Psalms. The title captures what the book as a whole deals with, namely, perseverance. Peterson says:

> We assume that if something can be done at all, it can be done quickly and efficiently. Our attention spans have been conditioned by thirty-second commercials. Our sense of reality has been flattened by thirty-page abridgements... It is not difficult in such a world to get a person interested in the message of the gospel; it is terrifically difficult to sustain the interest. Millions of people in our culture make decisions for Christ, but there is a dreadful attrition rate. Many claim to have been born again, but the evidence for mature Christian discipleship is slim. In our kind of culture anything, even news about God, can be sold if it is packaged freshly; but when it loses its novelty, it goes on the garbage heap. There is a great market for religious experience in our world; there is little enthusiasm for the patient acquisition of virtue, little inclination to sign up for a long apprenticeship in what earlier generations of Christians called holiness.[5]

~ ~ ~ ~ ~

"Patient acquisition of virtue" is a great descriptor for the Christian life. We may experience suffering and slander as well as a host of other difficulties, but as we remember the hope of the future we can persevere as we live a life of faithfulness on whatever bus routes we may find ourselves.

I also like how Peterson describes life on the other side of our rescue as a "long apprenticeship in what earlier generations of Christians called holiness." This parallels what Peter speaks of in verse 3: "You have had enough in the past of the evil things that godless people enjoy—their immorality and lust, their feasting and drunkenness and wild parties, and their terrible worship of idols" (I Peter 4:3, NLT). We need to move into a conviction of having had enough of evil things. There's a certain attitude of being done with what the world loves doing, regardless of what former friends might think. In other words, holiness takes a great amount of courage because it's a posture that believes what we choose not to do is as important as the things we choose to do. We give up behaviors. We put away childish things. We grow up and, in a real way, come to a time when we graduate out of a world that loves castes and abrasive, belittling behaviors. This is a long apprenticeship, and as such it demands persevering courage.

On the Other Side of Day 4:

Parable Principle: Courage and perseverance are first-cousins.

Scripture Memory Verse for the Week: *"If you are suffering in a manner that pleases God, keep on doing what is right, and trust your lives to the God who created you, for he will never fail you"* (I Peter 4:19, NLT).

Questions for Reflection:

1. At what times have you had to persevere in your life? What did those seasons teach you about faith?

2. Do you agree that to persevere you have to be able to hold onto a future hope? Why or why not?

3. Would you say the "patient acquisition of virtue" is a good descriptor of the Christian life?

4. In what ways are you willing to follow Jesus with a long obedience in the same direction?

5. Are there realities that could put a stop to your persevering love for Jesus? If so, what are they, and how could you learn to live faithfully in the midst of them?

Taking a Quack at It:

Take on a physical or mental challenge this week (within reason of course). Whether it's walking, swimming, biking, or jogging, reading, doing a crossword puzzle or tackling an unfinished project, consider the role of perseverance. Think about what it means to run out of steam, and what it takes to develop endurance. How does this shed light on our life in Jesus?

Day 5: "Courage to Praise"

> *14 So be happy when you are insulted for being a Christian, for then the glorious Spirit of God rests upon you. 15 If you suffer, however, it must not be for murder, stealing, making trouble, or prying into other people's affairs. 16 But it is no shame to suffer for being a Christian. Praise God for the privilege of being called by his name!*

I had just gotten it for my birthday and I finally felt a part of the crowd. Certainly the back-benchers would take notice, and perhaps I'd even be able to move a few benches towards the middle section of the bus where I could then posture for a real shot at a coveted back bench. It was black, shiny, and able to be turned to ear-popping decibels. It was a Walkman.

My coveted Walkman was not only my hoped-for means toward social acceptance, it was also my weapon of choice against the heavy metal that played each and every day on the bus. My older brothers made me tape cassettes filled with contemporary Christian music. This genre was a brand new thing at the time. Amy Grant and Michael W. Smith had just started their forays into the music industry where they took Christ-centered lyrics and put them to contemporary sounds. So "Burn in Hell" was no longer blaring in my ears. I was able to listen to the tunes of heaven.

For several weeks I got along great. I'd start up my music as I took my seat near the front of the bus and spend the remainder of the trip tuned out of the chaos around me and tuned into praise of God. It became my daily time with Jesus, and it enabled me to go into school humming the truths of my Sunday morning church experience as I headed to algebra or Spanish 101.

But like most everything in life, things unexpectedly changed one morning when a back-bencher turned his interest to what I was listening to. Up until that moment my Christian music was a private matter. I had been praising God silently and I wanted to keep it that way. I preferred it if the rest of the kids on the bus assumed I was listening to Quiet Riot or Led Zeppelin.

"Hey, Tim," Kenny asked. "What're ya listening to?"

"Uhhhh, nothing really." I said in embarrassment.

With hands reached out, the back-bencher asked to listen to my Walkman. I was ashamed. What'll he think?

He placed the headphones on his ears and listened for a moment or two. I wanted to crawl under my seat.

"Who you listening to? I don't think I've heard this group?"

"It's a new group," I said. "They just came out a couple of months ago. Their name is Petra."

"Petra? Never heard of them." He listened some more. "Did they just say the name 'Jesus'?"

He smirked as he continued to hear the song. I simply looked out the window, wanting the attention to come to a quick end. After several more moments he handed the headphones back to me. I felt like I needed to say something in my defense.

"They're sort of on the lines of Def Leppard. I'm sure they'll be on MTV sometime soon."

"I doubt it," Kenny said, rolling his eyes at me. He walked to the back of the bus and sat down. I quickly tucked my new Walkman into my back-

Rescued into a Life of Courage

pack and wondered why I had been so stupid as to bring it in the first place.

~ ~ ~ ~ ~

It's not hard to praise God when we're alone and by ourselves. It's not hard to praise God when we gather at church and join with numerous other people who share the same faith, the same attitude of worship and the same desire to draw close to Jesus. It's not hard to praise Jesus when we keep the tunes of our praise a private matter. It's quite another thing to praise God in the midst of back-benchers who smirk and furrow their brows in disbelief. In circumstances like that, praise can easily go from worship to tucking one's tunes of praise into a low-profile backpack.

~ ~ ~ ~ ~

Peter lived at a time when people not only smirked at worship of Jesus; they'd downright kill you for it. Yet Peter reminds the believers he's writing to be courageous in their praise of the Lord. "So be happy when you are insulted for being a Christian, for then the glorious Spirit of God rests upon you. If you suffer, however, it must not be for murder, stealing, making trouble, or prying into other people's affairs. But it is no shame to suffer for being a Christian. Praise God for the privilege of being called by his name" (I Peter 4:14–16, NLT).

Let's take a close look at what Peter is saying. "Be happy when you are insulted for being a Christian, for then the glorious Spirit of God rests upon you" (I Peter 4:14, NLT). Peter could relate to the position I took on Bus 90, because he took the very same one the night of Jesus' betrayal. When Jesus was being led away under armed guard and Peter was in the middle aisle of the courtyard being eyed suspiciously by numerous back-benchers, they asked Peter if he happened to have the tunes of Jesus in his Walkman. He downplayed and downright denied the questions three times. So Peter knew the feeling of insult and shame- avoidance. Further, he also understood the pain of the rooster's crow and how it overpowered the temporary respite he had from those who were trying to pry the headphones from him.

But Peter's desire to avoid insult and shame smacked up against the harsh reality that Jesus was courageously walking into it. For the joy set before him, as the author of the Letter to the Hebrews wrote, Jesus endured the cross and despised the shame. In other words, Jesus didn't give a lick about the shame this world heaps on those who listen to the tunes of heaven. Peter caught sight of how Jesus handled smirks and contemptuous eye-rolling and, as Peter rehearsed what he witnessed on Calvary, he must have somewhere along the line come to the conclusion that if God's Spirit rested on Jesus there on the cross, then God's Spirit most definitely seeks to rest on those men and women, who like their Savior, endure insults because they follow the beat of a different drum. "Be happy when you are insulted for being a Christian, for then the glorious Spirit of God rests upon you" (I Peter 4:14, NLT).

Peter also goes on to say that "if you suffer, however, it must not be for murder, stealing, making trouble, or prying into other people's affairs. But it is no shame to suffer for being a Christian. Praise God for the privilege of being called by his name" (I Peter 4:15–16, NLT)! Peter hammers home the point that there are two kinds of suffering. There's the suffering that comes as a result of sinful actions and there's the suffering that flows out of being a Christian. The two are not the same!

How often in ministry I come in contact with people who reflect the former reality. Pastoral care is requested because a person's selfish and sin-filled consequences are beginning to catch up with them and they are at a complete loss. Certainly there's a need for pastoral care, guidance and compassion; but we as the church have lost all sense of good and godly shame. There is a place to feel shame for sinful stuff. There's a place to weep when we realize the rooster's started crowing. There's a place to take intentional ownership for hiding our Walkmans and pretending that we don't listen to the tunes of the gospel when we're on our buses. Godly shame over things we need to feel shame about is a good thing.

What's ironic is how we often don't feel shame for our sin but we do feel shame for our faith in Jesus. We feel ashamed of our faith because the possibility of insults and the lack of acceptance of those on our bus route terrify us. We feel like we've got to have their approval so we can avoid suffering for being a Christian; yet Peter knows the truth on this matter. As he tucked his Walkman out of sight, he was confronted with the gaze of Jesus who was journeying to his crucifixion. Insults were hurled at this holy Son of God who knew no shame because of sin. He was spit on. Mocked. Clubbed. Scourged. Stripped of his clothing. Laughed at. Taunted. Left for dead. Every twisted kind of rejection, blasphemy and shame were heaped on Jesus. He took all of it and was totally alone in the process. No back-benchers had his back. No middle or front-benchers stood by his side. Even those who used to sit in the same bench with him now stood at a distance. And yet it was sheer joy to Jesus, because he knew that all of the shaming he had to endure would deal shame a deathblow. It would alter and forever change the equation. Shame would be made powerless because of the shame that Jesus endured. Further, in Jesus shame would become an opportunity for joy.

~ ~ ~ ~ ~

The Church needs to reclaim shame over sin and joy over being a Christian. **We need to rescue the truth that it is a privilege to be called by his name**. When the headphones are taken off of our ears by someone we really want to impress, we don't need to lie and say we're listening to the tunes of this world. We can actually say we are worshiping Jesus. When the smirks come and the eyes roll and feelings of rejection and shame begin to crowd in, we can go on listening to our Walkmans and actually smile as we look out the window—knowing full well that we're not sitting alone.

ON THE OTHER SIDE OF DAY 5:

Parable Principle: We need to rescue the truth that it is a privilege to be called by his name.

Scripture Memory Verse for the Week: *"If you are suffering in a manner that pleases God, keep on doing what is right, and trust your lives to the God who created you, for he will never fail you"* (I Peter 4:19, NLT).

Questions for Reflection:

1. Have you ever been ashamed of Jesus? Try to think back on the circumstances and situation of that experience.
2. Are there some areas in your life where you still try to hide the tunes of the Kingdom of God from the people around you? Why?
3. What would need to change in you for you to courageously praise Jesus, even if insults come your way?

4. Do you agree there's a good shame we need to experience in relationship to sin? Why or why not?

5. What happens inside of you when you consider that God's Spirit rests on those who are insulted because of their faith in Jesus? What does this say about God?

6. In what way(s) do you believe it's a privilege to be called by Jesus' name?

**Taking a Quack at It:**

If you find that you typically go with the crowd when it comes to workplace or peer-group conversations, try to begin to voice your own convictions about what you believe and how your faith in Jesus informs your life. See what the responses from those around you are and how those responses/reactions challenge you personally.

Day 6: "Courage to Trust"

> *19 So if you are suffering in a manner that pleases God, keep on doing what is right, and trust your lives to the God who created you, for he will never fail you.*

There were a few moments when I didn't dread riding on Bus 90. They were few and far between, but they still stick out in my memory. I remember those particular bus rides because I was able to be at complete rest. I didn't have to give one thought to what the back-benchers might do. I didn't have to worry if Rusty was looking for a victim or if Kenny was going to check up on what was playing in my Walkman. I could literally be myself and enjoy the ride even in the midst of the chaos. What made the difference in those moments was a relationship. A big brother relationship.

My oldest brother, Mike, sometimes sat with me on Bus 90. I'm not sure if he did so because there was a lack of seats at the time or if he sensed I needed a respite; but I would go into the window side part of the bench and Mike would sit between me and the aisle. Mike was four years older than me and he could pretty much sit wherever he wanted. Most of the kids on the bus either liked Mike or at the very least respected him. So when Mike sat next to me I was guaranteed a sense of peace and relief. The spit wads still might sail my way and the insults and bullying might very well continue, but the basic relational reality that everyone understood on the bus was that if someone wanted to mess with me they'd have to go through Mike first.

~ ~ ~ ~ ~

Our relationship with Jesus is a lot like my experience with my older brother. Jesus is our older brother, and he sits between us and a lot of things. Think about it. Jesus has taken away the sting of death. Death tried to mess with Jesus in order to continue to bully all the rest of us, and Jesus put a definite end to it. Jesus has also defeated sin and the curse of sin. The Evil One had slithered into the Garden of Eden at the beginning of creation and tried to snake his way back into things when Jesus dealt him a crushing blow. Now, for those who follow Jesus, sin has been rendered powerless, and we can actually will to love God and our neighbor.

Now consider this relational reality. If Jesus has taken away the sting of death and the power of sin, how much more can he also give us a rest from the kinds of fear and worry our chaotic bus rides so often create in us. Jesus is the Prince of Peace precisely because he brings peace to you and me if we share the bench we're in with him. This peace—this relational presence that Jesus brings—is all about the courage to trust. Peter says, "So if you are suffering in a manner that pleases God, keep on doing what is right, and trust your lives to the God who created you, for he will never fail you" (I Peter 4:19, NLT).

Repeat those final four words: "He will never fail you."

Remember, Peter is calling the recipients of his letter to have the courage to trust in God despite the kinds of circumstances that would terrify most of us. There was physical and relational persecution that many of these Christians had to endure. Nero was on the rise and he had deep contempt for Jesus' followers; he often exacted his fury with the kinds of acts that can only be described as horrific and inhumane. These were faithful people who had every reason to NOT trust, to walk away, to fade and disappear into the crowds. If there was ever a time to choose to stop following Jesus, these people could have made a pretty good case for it. It was a death sentence. Nevertheless, Peter relentlessly calls these recipients to trust God in the midst of their sufferings and to persevere in doing what pleases God.

~ ~ ~ ~ ~

We struggle with having the courage to trust God in the manner Peter is describing. It's easy to forget that Jesus is the Prince of Peace when everything around us is troubling. We do tend to trust Jesus for heaven (someday). We also trust Jesus out of necessity when we encounter things like illness, tragedy or events that are far from our ability to respond to or handle on our own. However, in terms of daily living, I am convinced many of us live as agnostics. We don't trust God in our jobs, families, bills, hobbies and difficulties. We don't trust God to be working in our chaotic circumstances because we've come to assume that if God is present, the difficulties and hardships should completely cease. When they don't come to a speedy end we look at Jesus who's sitting next to us and we wonder why the spit wads, insults and bullying still come our way. But **Jesus didn't come to stop hardship altogether; he came to be present to us in the midst of it.** *In* the valley of the shadow of death, you, Jesus, are with me.

~ ~ ~ ~ ~

I've come to learn that Jesus knows what he's doing with my life. I may not always understand why I'm getting hit in the back of the head with a spit wad or why my ear is getting flicked time after time after time... but I have slowly learned that even in the midst of the things I don't always grasp, I can trust Jesus. I can rest in his presence, knowing that he is sovereign and that nothing gets past him into where I'm sitting in my bench without going through him first. If something is hard to handle or causes a lot of fear and worry, I'm learning to look to Jesus and trust that he knows what he's doing with my life. Further, I'm learning to look for Jesus' footprint. Since he is the Prince of Peace, there is a certain inner peace that comes from being close to him. It's the kind of peace that enables us to live in the wisdom of Jesus who once said, "So don't worry about tomorrow, for tomorrow will bring its own worries. Today's trouble is enough for today" (Matthew 6:34, NLT). As we let go of worry we can begin to step into much needed rest. We can sleep in peace because the Lord watches over our lives. We can have hope for tomorrow because our eventual and eternal hope is in Jesus himself. We can sit next to Jesus and trust that our older brother is with us, even when everything in our daily reality screams that he isn't. We can have the courage to trust.

ON THE OTHER SIDE OF DAY 6:

Parable Principle: Jesus didn't come to stop hardship altogether; he came to be present to us in the midst of it.

Scripture Memory Verse for the Week: *"If you are suffering in a manner that pleases God, keep on doing what is right, and trust your lives to the God who created you, for he will never fail you"* (I Peter 4:19, NLT).

Questions for Reflection:

1. Have you ever been in the presence of someone who made you feel safe? Who was that person and what was that experience like?
2. Jesus' presence is sometimes best experienced in the midst of difficulty. Would you agree? Why or why not?
3. When have you continued to entrust your life to God even though the circumstances around you said you shouldn't? What was the outcome?
4. How have you experienced the peace of Jesus?
5. In what ways do you find rest on a weekly basis?
6. Would you say that trusting God requires a great amount of courage? Why or why not?

Taking a Quack at It:

Take some time to look up scripture passage that deal with peace. What do you notice as common themes? What comforts you? What do you find difficult or troubling about trusting God? What area(s) of your life is God calling you to entrust to him? What would it take to do so?

DAY 7: REST

Worship in community.

Enjoy the presence of loved ones.

Take time to take note of God's creation.

Reflect on this past week.

Commit this coming week to the Lord.

ENDNOTES

1 Cf., Timothy Farrell, *Braveheart Pastors: The Role of Courage In a Pastor's Ability to Lead the Local Church Effectively*. Ann Arbor, MI: ProQuest-CSA, LLC., 2007.

2 Thomas Aquinas, *Sumae Theologia*. Vol. 42. Transl. Anthony Ross and P.G. Walsh. New York: McGraw; London: Eyre and Spottiswoode, 1966, p. 13.

3 E. Stanley Jones: Quoted in Donald Demaray and C. Reginald Johnson, *Spiritual Formation for Christian Leaders: Lessons from the Life and Teaching of E. Stanley Jones*. Nashville, TN: Abingdon Press, 2007.

4 Eugene Peterson, *The Message: The Bible in Contemporary Language*. Colorado Springs, CO: NavPress, 2002, p. 2214.

5 Eugene Peterson, *A Long Obedience in the Same Direction*. Downers Grove, IL: InterVarsity Press, 2000, p. 16.

PARABLE 5

Sweaty Starfish:
Rescued into a Life of Preparedness

I was never much of an athlete in school. I lacked the aggression to win and conquer an opponent. So the day I was asked to showcase wrestling skills in fourth-grade gym class became about one of the lowest points of my elementary school career. I was totally unprepared.

The room was filled with wall-to-wall padding on the floor. My classmates and I were decked out in knee high tube socks, short shorts and screened t-shirts. We had just entered a four-week tour that would take us through the world of wrestling. Whether we liked it or not, we would be learning how to assume offensive and defensive wrestling postures and how to pin our opponents in either position. I was dreading the entire month and hoped I could sort of fly under the radar of my gym teacher and not have to give much effort.

My hopes were pulled out from under me on the very first day of class. No sooner had we entered the wrestling arena than Mr. Cornick called my name and asked me to come to the center of the room. I couldn't believe my ears. Out of all of the athletes who lined the walls of the room, I was called on. Mr. Cornick then asked me to assume the defensive position. Trying to keep my backside out of sight, I got on all fours. Once I was in place the teacher named my opponent. Fred was asked to join me in the center of the room. I was shocked. Fred was an out-and-out athlete of athletes. He played every sport imaginable with skill and confidence. He was strong, aggressive and unafraid. He took the offensive posture and I knew I had only one choice: I had to do the unthinkable. I had to revert to the only homemade wrestling move I knew, the "starfish."

I had first come up with the starfish position as a defensive move against my two older brothers. It was simple but effective. I dropped down onto my stomach, stretched all four limbs straight out and let my weight keep me from being flipped over onto my back.

When Mr. Cornick blew his beloved whistle, Fred began to try to twist my frame and fold me into a ball and pin me on my back. I simply did the starfish. As my classmates laughed in disbelief, I held my position for a good five minutes. Fred attempted to lift my torso, move my head, pull my arms back, pry my legs over, he tried every conceivable move, but I refused to budge. As Fred gave me a good working-over and I began to pour sweat, a vacuum seal developed between the padding on the floor and my drenched belly button. I could not be turned over and pinned. The class laughed... Fred was exhausted... I was a bit embarrassed... but I was unmoved. Mr. Cornick just shook his head.

~ ~ ~ ~ ~

When it comes to athletics and physical training, some of us feel like starfish more than we do competitors. I went into that gym class knowing only one move. So the result for me was that I wasted time lying on my stomach like a starfish—confused, still, suctioned. A lot of times we have this same experience when it comes to our faith. We are one-trick ponies (or in this case, starfish). That's why I love what Paul says to his young student, Timothy. He states in I Timothy 4:8–9, "'Physical training is good, but training for godliness is much better, promising benefits in this life and in the life to come.' This is a trustworthy saying, and everyone should accept it" (NLT). Paul is quoting what must have been a well-known phrase at the time. It's a truth we would do well to follow ourselves.

~ ~ ~ ~ ~

Our family believes in physical fitness. We attend a local fitness center and try to get there three times a week. Tracey and I want to be healthy and we desire that our kids be healthy too. But there is a difference between wanting to be physically healthy and wanting to look perfect. Now the two may go together naturally, but if concern over how our exterior looks to others becomes our core passion, we can easily become overly concerned with physical training to the detriment of time spent in godly training.

How many families and churches are as concerned with training in godliness as they are with physical training? If we spend three times a week working our bodies into health, are we also spending intentional time working our godliness into health?

~ ~ ~ ~ ~

The Apostle Paul makes it clear that training in godliness has greater benefits than physical training because it "benefits in this life and in the life to come" (I Timothy 4:8, NLT). Notice that Paul is affirming the role of physical training—it does benefit us and we're wise to pursue it— but whenever we give effort to growing in godliness we are making a difference in how we live in the here and now and in the life to come. In other words, training in godliness has far-reaching effects that physical training can't provide. And here's the cool thing: You don't have to be an athlete to grow in godliness. You can be the most uncoordinated person there is, and God can work in you the kind of godly strength that'll enable you to become spiritually strong. My hope is that this week's material will give you a good start in this direction as you live on the other side of your rescue. Further, I've placed this particular material here because the further we get from the experience of our rescue the more prone we are to become weary and to lose the momentum we had at the start of our journey with Jesus. We're tempted to lose hope and fall flat on our stomachs. But this is really the time and opportunity to become intentional. To pursue Jesus not because we feel like it, but because we choose to be faithful.

So I challenge you to get out of the starfish position. I encourage you to begin to hold training in godliness as a personal priority in your life so that you won't feel like I did in gym class, completely unprepared for the wrestling match I found myself in.

BIBLICAL TEXT FOR WEEK 5: HEBREWS 12:1–17

1 Therefore, since we are surrounded by such a huge crowd of witnesses to the life of faith, let us strip off every weight that slows us down, especially the sin that so easily trips us up. And let us run with endurance the race God has set before us. 2 We do this by keeping our eyes on Jesus, the champion who initiates and perfects our faith. Because of the joy awaiting him, he endured the cross, disregarding its shame. Now he is seated in the place of honor beside God's throne. 3 Think of all the hostility he endured from sinful people; then you won't become weary and give up. 4 After all, you have not yet given your lives in your struggle against sin.

5 And have you forgotten the encouraging words God spoke to you as his children? He said,

> "My child, don't make light of the Lord's discipline,
>   and don't give up when he corrects you.
> 6 For the Lord disciplines those he loves,
>   and he punishes each one he accepts as his child."

7 As you endure this divine discipline, remember that God is treating you as his own children. Who ever heard of a child who is never disciplined by its father? 8 If God doesn't discipline you as he does all of his children, it means that you are illegitimate and are not really his children at all. 9 Since we respected our earthly fathers who disciplined us, shouldn't we submit even more to the discipline of the Father of our spirits, and live forever?

10 For our earthly fathers disciplined us for a few years, doing the best they knew how. But God's discipline is always good for us, so that we might share in his holiness. 11 No discipline is enjoyable while it is happening—it's painful! But afterward there will be a peaceful harvest of right living for those who are trained in this way.

12 So take a new grip with your tired hands and strengthen your weak knees. 13 Mark out a straight path for your feet so that those who are weak and lame will not fall but become strong.

14 Work at living in peace with everyone, and work at living a holy life, for those who are not holy will not see the Lord. 15 Look after each other so that none of you fails to receive the grace of God. Watch out that no poisonous root of bitterness grows up to trouble you, corrupting many. 16 Make sure that no one is immoral or godless like Esau, who traded his birthright as the firstborn son for a single meal. 17 You know that afterward, when he wanted his father's blessing, he was rejected. It was too late for repentance, even though he begged with bitter tears.

Day 1: "Prepared to Endure"

> *1 Therefore, since we are surrounded by such a huge crowd of witnesses to the life of faith, let us strip off every weight that slows us down, especially the sin that so easily trips us up. And let us run with endurance the race God has set before us. 2 We do this by keeping our eyes on Jesus, the champion who initiates and perfects our faith. Because of the joy awaiting him, he endured the cross, disregarding its shame. Now he is seated in the place of honor beside God's throne. 3 Think of all the hostility he endured from sinful people; then you won't become weary and give up. 4 After all, you have not yet given your lives in your struggle against sin.*

It was a cold fall day in upstate New York, and I was on the track and field part of our high school's campus. I had never stepped foot on the track before. The feel of the gravel and the sight of the oval track were brand new to me. I had also never been timed before. I knew I could run pretty fast, but I also knew that my two older brothers had been born with natural speed. I had always lumbered more than ran. But there I was, lined up with about eight other students from gym class, competing to see who could run the 100-yard dash in the fastest time. My heart was pumping. My legs were antsy. I was ready to move.

The air-horn blew and I felt like Wile E. Coyote on Looney Tunes. My legs were moving at 100 mph, but it seemed like it took a moment or two to gain traction. Finally I was off and running. Three or four older kids who were already involved in track were a little distance out in front of me. I wondered if I could catch up. As I ran along I found that I was feeling a little odd about the idea of being timed. I wasn't so sure I liked the notion of receiving a time at the finish of the race, because I was afraid it would be discouraging. But then it happened. After we rounded the first curve I realized I wasn't as far behind as I thought I would be. In fact, I was still on the heels of the more wiry students in front of me. I couldn't believe it!   As we began to near the last stretch of the race I looked into the eyes of the coaches. I noticed that they were watching us... me... and their eyes reflected looks of encouragement. It was kind of like one of those moments when someone's demeanor speaks louder than any amount of words can. I felt like they were saying, "Come on, Tim, you can do this." Their witness of my race made my legs keep moving despite the burn and the pain. I wanted to live up to their expectations so badly that I pushed myself and actually passed one of the runners who had been in front of me. When I crossed the finish line I was third, but it really felt like I had won. I knew if I had been left to myself I would have given up halfway through the race; but with the others racing with me and the coaches looking on, I put out a whole lot more effort than I ever thought possible.

~ ~ ~ ~ ~

The gospel is opposed to earning, but it is not opposed to effort. In fact, members of the early Church understood themselves to be the athletes of God. They recognized that effort can be a good thing when it comes to growing in godliness, and they were willing to work their hardest toward that end. It's in this spirit that the author of the Letter to the Hebrews says, "Therefore, since we are surrounded by such a huge crowd of witnesses to the life of faith, let us strip off every weight that slows us down, especially the sin that so easily trips us up. And let us run with endurance the race God has set before us" (Hebrews 12:1, NLT).

The author of Hebrews states that we are surrounded. Surrounded by whom? Surrounded by a huge crowd of witnesses to the life of faith. A sampling of these witnesses is mentioned in chapter 11. Suffice it to say they were men and women who knew what it meant to run hard. They had developed strong legs of faith and knew what it was like to feel sore and tired. Some had even given their very lives to God in their own personal races.

This crowd of witnesses empathizes with those of us who are now in the thick of the race. The author says they surround us and cheer us on. Further, as we look to how they raced in their lives, we are emboldened to run in a similar way. As we rehearse and remember their accounts of faith, we find ourselves looking at how to be as faithful as they once were. We take notice of the speed of their obedience and the quick footwork of their holy dispositions and we begin to have some parameters as to what sins we're currently carrying that, if we stripped them off, would free us up to run even faster.

The author also points out that we are to run with endurance: "Let us run with endurance the race God has set before us" (Hebrews 12:1b, NLT). This is a wise word because I often see people sprint the race God has set before us. I think we tend to sprint, because we easily lose sight of the fact that the race we're in is one God has set before us. To sprint is to reveal that I really want this race to get over with quickly. I want to be done with God's race, so I can get on with another race on another track. But when we consider that the race we're in is God's—and that he is worthy of our best and our all—we are able to develop a longing for that runner's second wind that gives endurance. This race is worth running our whole life long.

So how do we get this second wind—this kind of endurance? Well, all of you runners know full well that running with endurance doesn't just happen. Endurance comes out of intentional effort. The intentional effort that gives us endurance comes out of "keeping our eyes on Jesus, the champion who initiates and perfects our faith" (Hebrews 12:2a, NLT). Keeping our eyes on Jesus is like the experience I had of taking notice of the coaches. I kept my eyes on the coaches, and the result was that I experienced encouragement to stay in the race. It helped prepare me to endure.

When we keep our eyes on Jesus we get that kind of encouragement. Why? Because we see how he endured. "Because of the joy awaiting him, he endured the cross, disregarding its shame. Now he is seated in the place of honor beside God's throne. Think of all the hostility he endured from sinful people; then you won't become weary and give up" (Hebrews 12:2b, NLT). Oftentimes we get weary and give up in our race of faith because we fail to consider Jesus. We look only at our limited experience, our pain or our circumstances, and we lose hope. All we see is ourselves. But **when we keep our eyes on Jesus, we'll always be encouraged because we'll never match the painful race he had to run.**

Jesus' race has no equal because he didn't have to run in the first place. He had no ownership of our failings and our sins. He was spotless and in glory with his Father. Yet he was willing to give "up his divine privileges; he took the humble position of a slave and was born as a human being. When he appeared in human form, he humbled himself in obedience to God and died a criminal's death on a cross" (Philippians 2:7–8, NLT). However painful any of our races might become, they'll always pale in comparison to Jesus' matchless race. He ran when he didn't have to, out of sheer love, to win for you and me the victory through his own painful and obedient effort. With that kind of example in my Savior, I could run all day long, couldn't you?

So let's consider Jesus and, as we do so, let's be reminded that however tired and sore you and I might be, we haven't "yet given [our] lives in [our] struggle against sin" (Hebrews 12:4, NLT). In other words, there's still some more racing to be done. There's still some more effort to be exerted. Let's keep our eyes on Jesus and be prepared to keep running!

On the Other Side of Day 1:

Parable Principle: When we keep our eyes on Jesus, we'll always be encouraged because we'll never match the painful race he had to run.

Scripture Memory Verse for the Week: *"Let us run with endurance the race God has set before us" (Hebrews 12:1b, NLT).*

Questions for Reflection:

1. Have you ever been in a race before? If so, what helped and what hindered you? How were you encouraged to complete that race?
2. Would you agree the race of faith requires endurance? Why? Why not?
3. What person from the Bible encourages you the most when you consider the "race" he/she ran? What about their race helps you to run yours?
4. Are sins weighing you down in terms of your ability to run the race God has set before you? How can you strip them off?
5. How do you look to Jesus in your life? Name some practical ways you do this during the week.

Taking a Quack at It:

Ask the Lord to help you discern what areas of your life you've become weary in. Talk with the Lord about those areas and ask for his help in developing endurance in them.

Day 2: "God's Effort"

> 5 And have you forgotten the encouraging words God spoke to you as his children? He said,
>
> > "My child, don't make light of the Lord's discipline,
> >   and don't give up when he corrects you.
> > 6 For the Lord disciplines those he loves,
> >   and he punishes each one he accepts as his child."
>
> 7 As you endure this divine discipline, remember that God is treating you as his own children. Who ever heard of a child who is never disciplined by its father? 8 If God doesn't discipline you as he does all of his children, it means that you are illegitimate and are not really his children at all. 9 Since we respected our earthly fathers who disciplined us, shouldn't we submit even more to the discipline of the Father of our spirits, and live forever?
>
> 10 For our earthly fathers disciplined us for a few years, doing the best they knew how. But God's discipline is always good for us, so that we might share in his holiness. 11 No discipline is enjoyable while it is happening—it's painful! But afterward there will be a peaceful harvest of right living for those who are trained in this way.

All of life is a response to God. God is the initiator. God enables and empowers. God gifts and uses you and me and, as a result, our efforts are simply a loving response to all God has already done. We get in trouble when we fail to recognize God's loving effort and move forward with our own efforts. We may get along just fine for a season of time, but eventually we'll be flat on our stomachs just trying to get by without being pinned. The reason for this is when our effort is the starting point, we are unable to both see and receive the kind of love God offers us. His love is what fuels our life in Jesus and helps us to be prepared to live for him.

Amy Carmichael, missionary and author, once said, "God wants lovers. Oh, how tepid is the love of so many who call themselves by His name. How tepid is our own—my own—in comparison with the lava fires of his eternal love. I pray that you may be an ardent lover, the kind of lover who sets others on fire."[1] To become a lover of God can at times require our own efforts to draw near to God. However, I want to underscore the initiative of God and point out the effort he continuously makes to draw us near to himself. His effort is the primary way we grow in our love for him. His efforts are eternally greater and more substantial than our own. To acknowledge this and to receive the truth of it is to move in the direction of a healthy personal effort in our life with Jesus.

So how does God exert effort in your life and my life? Well, there are certainly countless ways in which he does so (many that we can name and possibly even more that we aren't even aware of); but the one we'll focus on today comes out of our biblical text for this week: "My child, don't make light of the Lord's discipline, and don't give up when he corrects you. For the Lord disciplines those he loves, and he punishes each one he accepts as his child" (Hebrews 12:5b–6, NLT).

God's discipline is central to how he exhibits love for you and me. The wording the author of Hebrews uses here is that of instructor to child. God is the instructor and we are his children who are being corrected. If you've ever been an instructor to children or had to discipline a son or a daughter, you know the kind of effort that goes into it and how it's rooted in love for the child. Further, the discipline being referred to is the hardships and sufferings the recipients have had to face and will continue to experience. Their outward circumstances of pain are a way in which God is training them and preparing them to become more like Jesus.

~ ~ ~ ~ ~

When I was suctioned to the floor in my starfish position during gym class, I was exerting all sorts of effort and getting nowhere fast. I was simply trying to stay alive while Fred worked his understanding of the sport of wrestling on my sweat-drenched frame. I was embarrassed, humiliated and angry. Although Mr. Cornick was using our demo to introduce the sport to the class, I wished I could have gone into the demonstration more prepared so that I could have at least competed. Outside correction would have given me a foothold to at least gain a sense of confidence in that difficult circumstance.

~ ~ ~ ~ ~

Whether we are in gym class or anywhere else in life, all of us need discipline. It brings health and wholeness. It gives insight and allows us to gain understanding. With discipline we can course-correct for the purpose of enduring with dignity the efforts we are giving. The same holds true for our life in Jesus. God disciplines us for the sake of instruction and correction. He wants you and me to be prepared to live the life of Jesus with confidence so that we're not stuck on some floor somewhere holding on for dear life. Oftentimes this kind of discipline comes our way through the painful and difficult realities we're in the midst of and having to endure.

The text goes on to say, "As you endure this divine discipline, remember that God is treating you as his own children" (Hebrews 12:7a, NLT). When God disciplines, we have a tendency to want to walk away. It would be odd to anticipate and enjoy discipline, so it makes sense that we have a hard time with it; but we are called to "endure this divine discipline."

How do we endure? We endure by understanding that when God disciplines us, he is really treating us like his own children. This begs the question: Who are God's own children? The best example of God's children being disciplined for the purpose of drawing close to God is the people of Israel throughout the the Old Testament. If you have time, peruse those pages and look upon account after account of difficulties, hardships, trials and tests, and see how God used those very circumstances to train his children. He disciplined them because he loved them. He corrected them because he wanted them to be close to him and his ways and purposes.

Take some time to think about any of your own difficult circumstances. As you reflect, open yourself to how God may be using these realities to correct and prepare you. Now bear in mind that I'm NOT saying God causes all the pain, tragedy and brokenness we encounter. I am pointing to the ability of God to use all of that stuff to love us as his children. And here's the thing: The author of Hebrews understands the reality of discipline and suffering. He says, "But God's discipline is always good for us, so that we might share in his holiness. No discipline is enjoyable while it is happening—it's painful! But afterward there will be a peaceful harvest of right living for those who are trained in this way" (Hebrews 12:10b–11, NLT).

God's effort for you and me—his discipline—*is always good*. Further, God's discipline can be good and yet NOT enjoyable. It can even be downright painful. God can train us in ways that cause tears, feelings of hopelessness, anger, attitudes of resistance, fear, frustration and more! But we have to keep the end in mind: "Afterward there will be a peaceful harvest of right living for those who are trained in this way" (Hebrews 12:11b, NLT). When God disciplines, he lovingly breaks us down. We become pliable, moldable, teachable. We turn into disciples. It's only in this kind of posture on the other side of our rescue that we can reap the harvest of right living.

It's kind of like an unruly team a coach takes under his wings. The team is full of pride. The members of the team are unteachable, and they want to do their own thing rather than run the plays the coach has in mind. Such a team will only come to the place of being broken enough to listen and receive the coach's instruction after they've gone through the pain and difficulty of losing a series of games. It's in the bitter reality of hardship that the coach can then course-correct and prepare the team to play effectively in the future.

Have we been trained in this way? Have we paused in our own efforts long enough to see *God's* efforts in our lives? He is initiating us into life with him. *He* is instructing and correcting you and me. Often this kind of loving discipline comes through the painful realities of life. We may not like the pain but, if we commit to endure, there will come a time and a place when peacefulness will invade our lives because we are living close to the heart of God. God loves us and in every way he has taken the first step to work his loving efforts into your life and mine. No matter how long we've been stretched out on the floor feeling helpless, we can now stand and face the difficulties we wrestle with, knowing that God is working on our behalf.

On the Other Side of Day 2:

Parable Principle: When our effort is the starting point, we are unable to both see and receive the kind of love God offers us.

Scripture Memory Verse for the Week: *"Let us run with endurance the race God has set before us" (Hebrews 12:1b, NLT).*

Questions for Reflection:

1. Would you agree that God is always the initiator? Why or why not? How have you experienced this in your life?

Rescued into a Life of Preparedness

2. Why is God's discipline important to our growth in godliness? What has this looked like in your life?

3. The author of Hebrews talks about a "harvest of right living" when we are trained in God's discipline. What do you think the author means by this statement?

4. Has there been a time you've tried to live for God in your own effort? How'd it turn out? Would you agree God's effort is greater than ours? If so, why and how has this been the case for you?

Taking a Quack at It:

Take some time to think of an experience when you had discipline and correction in your life and it helped you. In contrast, consider the opposite kind of memory—when you didn't have any instruction and the lack of it made you completely unprepared to handle a difficulty you faced. Try to apply these reflections to your life with Jesus.

Day 3: "Renewed"

12 So take a new grip with your tired hands and strengthen your weak knees.

I remember just lying there on the gym floor mat, completely exhausted. The demo was done and Fred was literally off of my back. My peers were laughing at this now rolled-over and sweaty starfish. I felt like I would never be able to lift myself up and return to my place as a wallflower (wallstarfish) among my peers. Further, I couldn't imagine making another effort when it came to the sport of wrestling. I was done with it.

~ ~ ~ ~ ~

I have sat down with dozens of men and women over the years that have come for pastoral care due to the fact that they are exhausted, sweaty starfish. They went into life with Jesus untrained and they wrestled with all of their effort; they have since come out on the other side wanting to simply return to their places as wall-starfish in the community of faith, looking to never make another effort in their life with

Jesus. They're done with it.

This reality of exhaustion in our life with Christ has been defined as a kind of "dark night of the soul" by Christian mystics and monastic communities. They are times when we feel spent, alone and done with following Jesus. I am convinced we all encounter these seasons from time to time, and so it's not surprising to me how often we experience it and how uncomfortable it can make us feel about ourselves, God and the integrity of our faith. Yet we need to understand it's a natural part of our growth and relationship with Jesus. If we can endure these seasons we will actually find ourselves closer to Jesus than before. So for those of us who are lying on our respective mats wondering if we can ever move again, we are called to hear and receive these words of encouragement: "So take a new grip with your tired hands and strengthen your knees" (Hebrews 12:12, NLT).

God calls us to a renewed effort. How does this renewal happen? Well, according to day two of this week (take a look back if you need to), it comes from redefining suffering and hardship. You see, those wrestling matches we loath are God's way of forming us in right living (cf. Hebrews 12:11). In other words, we don't grow sitting quietly by a wall. **We grow in godliness through the working-over we experience that leads us sweaty-starfish to total dependency on the Lord**. This famous verse from the Apostle Paul reflects this approach: "That's why I take pleasure in my weaknesses, and in the insults, hardships, persecutions, and troubles that I suffer for Christ. For when I am weak, then I am strong" (2 Corinthians 12:10, NLT).

Do you see the shift one of the greatest Christian wrestlers of all time made in his own life? Paul began to take pleasure in his weaknesses. This isn't a masochistic thing. This is the realization that our lack of ability is God's ability. Our weakness is God's time for strength. Our hardships, persecutions, troubles—all of it as a result of following Christ—are not reasons to be done with Jesus, but opportunities to seize and hold onto the truth that when we are weak we are strong. This is what it means to be renewed and to draw closer to Jesus.

Notice how the author of Hebrews words the verse for today. He doesn't say to take a new grip with our rested hands or to strengthen our already strong knees. He says, "Take a new grip with your tired hands and strengthen your weak knees" (Hebrews 12:12, NLT). God wants us to recognize how weak, sore and hurting we are. Further, as we accept our weakness and open ourselves to God's strength, our effort turns into the dynamic of God's effort through our weakness. This is how we can take a new grip and become strengthened.

~ ~ ~ ~ ~

I was able to return to the wrestling match. I came back to the padded floor humbled, sore and feeling quite weak. But the funny thing was that I was now ready to receive the coach's instructions. I learned that the worst thing you can do is become a starfish. I also learned that the best thing you can do is to learn the insights of the coach and follow his lead on how to face an opponent. Although I never won an actual match, it turned out that I was able to put up quite a fight. In the process, I accepted the truth that I could be renewed and get into the lessons. I would have missed out on quite a lot if I had stayed by the wall.

ON THE OTHER SIDE OF DAY 3:

Parable Principle: We grow in godliness through the working-over we experience that leads us sweaty-starfish to total dependency on the Lord.

Scripture Memory Verse for the Week: *"Let us run with endurance the race God has set before us"* (Hebrews 12:1b, NLT).

Questions for Reflection:

1. Name a time in your life when you felt like a sweaty starfish.

2. Have you ever gone through a dark night of the soul? Where are you in relation to it now?

3. Why is it so important to be open to a renewal of effort in your life with Jesus?

4. Do you agree it's important to accept your weakness and to be receptive to the Lord's strength?

5. How will things change in your life if you allow your effort to really become God's effort through you?

Taking a Quack at It:

Take some time to acknowledge what your tired hands and weak knees are. Be candid with God about these areas of exhaustion and ask the Lord to become your strength. Also, take the Apostle Paul's statement out of 2 Corinthians 12:10 and write it down on a slip of paper that you can carry with you. Refer to it throughout the day.

Day 4: "Prepared to be Selfless"

13 Mark out a straight path for your feet so that those who are weak and lame will not fall but become strong.

One of the ways we trained for wrestling in Mr. Cornick's gym class was to work on developing our legs and lungs through running. He'd open the gym door to the fields behind the school, the whistle would blow and we'd be off running. The first circuit around the cross-country track was the toughest for those of us who weren't familiar with the terrain. It was easy to lose footing, to trip or twist an ankle. But after the first lap it became a little easier, as we grew to understand the landscape and knew where to look out for woodchuck holes or thick tree roots.

~ ~ ~ ~ ~

The landscape the recipients of this Letter to the Hebrews traveled on was a lot like the cross-country track I ran on in gym class. It could sometimes be quite treacherous and difficult to travel on. Outside of the Roman road system, most passages and roads had twists and turns that could be harrowing and treacherous. The author of Hebrews springboards off of this reality when he says, "Mark out a straight path for your feet" (Hebrews 12:13a, NLT).

The recipients of the letter would have known exactly what the insight meant. They would have thought of the countless times they had lost their footing or seen a traveling loved one injured during the course of a journey. They would have made the connection between their actual experiences on paths and roads and the wisdom of intentionally marking out a sound path to journey on. Further, they would have seen how

Rescued into a Life of Preparedness

the need to do the same thing in one's journey of faith would be all-important.

The connection is a little more difficult for you and for me. We travel on smooth roads. Journeys for us are mostly uneventful. But for those of us who have jogged on an outdoor cross-country track, we can certainly catch the meaning of the need and wisdom for marking out a straight path for our feet. The primary way we mark out a straight path in our lives with Jesus is through study and meditation on the Bible. This same author of Hebrews says, "The word of God is alive and powerful. It is sharper than the sharpest two-edged sword, cutting between soul and spirit, between joint and marrow. It exposes our innermost thoughts and desires. Nothing in all of creation is hidden from God. Everything is naked and exposed before his eyes, and he is the one to whom we are accountable" (Hebrews 4:12–13, NLT). The Bible is the straight edge that marks out the path we are called to run on. The Bible is the plumb-line that evenly balances the road we're on. It's the guardrail. It's the glowing signage that warns of treacherous roads or hazardous conditions. Without the Bible, we are powerless to effectively understand the kind of life God is calling us to live and how to mark out that path before our feet.

As we accept the importance of God's Word and open our lives to it, the Spirit of God begins to prepare us to understand the straight path we are called to travel on. Jesus once said, "If you love me, obey my commandments. And I will ask the Father, and he will give you another Advocate, who will never leave you. He is the Holy Spirit, who leads into all truth" (John 14:15–17a, NLT). The Holy Spirit leads us into truth. Truth is how God calls and prepares us to live a life like Jesus. It's the intentional understanding of where to step and where to avoid stepping. It's the wisdom to travel in a way that doesn't lead us down treacherous paths.

~ ~ ~ ~ ~

One of the things I appreciated most when running the cross-country track were the friends I had, who both ran in front of me and told me when to watch out for a spot in the track that might trip me up. They might call back, "Watch that root" or "Keep an eye on the low hanging branches up ahead." With that input I was able to avoid getting hurt.

Looking out for the weaker person is what I love about the verse for today. "Mark out a straight path for your feet so that those who are weak and lame will not fall but become strong" (Hebrews 12:13, NLT). What the author is saying is that the effort we make to journey down a straight path with the Lord has an influencing effect in the lives of those who travel on our heels. In other words, our effort becomes a preparation of sorts to give selfless effort as we direct our learning of where the foot holes are to the weak and the lame behind us.

Now here's the thing: We have to consider who the weak and the lame are. Certainly the writer is not speaking literally. This is a path with the Lord, not a cross-country track in upstate New York. So when we consider for a moment the implications of who the author is referring to, we can't assume it's the people who are physically disabled. What the author is saying is quite remarkable. The weak and the lame are the people who have tried to run on their own and gotten injured and hurt in the process. It's the runners who've messed up and fallen into the woodchuck holes and twisted their ankles on the upturned roots. These are the relationally broken people we encounter. These are the ones we'd just as easily forget and leave in the dust. These are the people we might define as weak in their life with God. They don't see where to step or understand how to avoid injury.

So there's a principle in this text for the day: **My ability to run the race of faith is not just about me. It's about being prepared to help the people who may be lagging behind me to both navigate and effectively run their race of faith.** This is a call to a selfless effort of thinking about the weak and the lame. I am responsible to see them overcome their injuries and become strong. "Mark out a straight path for your feet so that those who are weak and lame will not fall but become strong" (Hebrews 12:13, NLT).

Do you think about the people running behind you? Do you consider the effort God has taken in your life to help you navigate the race of faith? If so, how are you doing the same for the weak and the lame who are trying to keep up with you?

~ ~ ~ ~ ~

In the 1992 Olympics in Barcelona, Derek Redmond was in the midst of a 400 semifinal heat. He had been running in such a way that he'd make the finals. As Derek hit the 175-meter mark from finishing the race, he heard a "pop" and felt intense pain. He had injured his right hamstring. Slowing down to a one-legged hop, he fell down on the track.

Derek's dad, Jim Redmond, who was up in the spectator stands, saw what had happened and began to run to his son. The medical crew arrived to carry Derek off the track but he refused. To everyone's amazement, he lifted himself to his feet and began to hobble towards the finish line. Derek's father finally reached his side, wrapped his arm around his son's waist and helped him walk toward the finish line. A couple of steps prior to finishing the race, Jim let go of his son and let Derek cross the line on his own. Together, on the other side of the finish line, they embraced and cried.

This image out of the 1992 Olympics is what it means to live into Hebrews 12:13. Like Jim Redmond, we are to come alongside those who are weak and lame and help them become strong again. Our selfless efforts are for the purpose of assisting those who are hurting to be able to finish the race of faith.

ON THE OTHER SIDE OF DAY 4:

Parable Principle: My ability to run the race of faith is about being prepared to help the people who may be lagging behind me to both navigate and effectively run their race of faith.

Scripture Memory Verse for the Week: *"Let us run with endurance the race God has set before us" (Hebrews 12:1b, NLT).*

Questions for Reflection:

1. Has there been someone in your life of faith who has helped you stay clear of hurt and injury? If so, name that person and how they have helped.

2. How is God's Word helping you to mark out a straight path for your feet?

3. God's effort through the Holy Spirit is critical to our journey of faith. In what ways have you experienced the Holy Spirit's help?

4. Who are the people who are running on your heels right now? What are some ways you can give selflessly to help them avoid footfalls and injury?

Taking a Quack at It:

Name a person or two you're willing to help in their race of faith. Make sure there are appropriate relational boundaries first (e.g., don't assist a person of the opposite sex in a way that would cross marital or ethical boundaries). Determine to check in on that person and pray for him/her. Make it a point to share (as it's appropriate) lessons you've learned that may help them to avoid becoming weak or lame.

Day 5: "Prepared to Work"

> *14 Work at living in peace with everyone, and work at living a holy life, for those who are not holy will not see the Lord.*

One of the most interesting things I learned in Mr. Cornick's wrestling class was that we didn't spend all of our time wrestling. This realization first came to me about midway through a series of sit-ups we were asked to do. I was close to seeing my breakfast for the second time, when Mr. Cornick stopped the class and talked with us about the importance of hard work. He said that good wrestling abilities came out of intentional work that focused on strengthening different parts of the body. As we worked on stomach muscles, leg muscles, arm and chest muscles, we were preparing ourselves to be able to compete on the wrestling mat. Although we griped and complained about our sit-ups and pull-ups, Mr. Cornick reminded us that when we came to his class, we needed to be prepared to work.

~ ~ ~ ~ ~

Like Mr. Cornick's gym class, we need to remember the importance of hard work in our life with Jesus. Now before you go griping and complaining, think for a moment on this. Do the teachings of Jesus come naturally to you and me? Is it easy to live the kind of life we've been going over these past five weeks? I'll speak for myself and say the life of Jesus works the kinds of muscles I didn't even know I had. I find myself getting sore, tired and relationally sick to my stomach. I'd much rather hold a grudge. I'd certainly enjoy disparaging speech over keeping my mouth shut when it comes to someone who's hurt me. I'd pursue self-

Rescued into a Life of Preparedness

gain as opposed to serving the person who's lagging behind me. You see, if we're honest we'd agree it does take hard work to live the life God's prepared for us to live. This is why Peter says, "Work at living in peace with everyone, and work at living a holy life" (Hebrews 12:14, NLT).

Neither of these comes easily or naturally.

~ ~ ~ ~ ~

What's interesting about the word "work" is you can also translate it with the word "pursue." **To pursue something is to take the initiative, because there's something of great value we're after.** The author of Hebrews is naming two things we need to see as having great value and worth: peace with people and holiness of life. Peace with people is the relational reality we experience around us. It's the visible and tangible relationships we encounter and maintain. On the other hand, holiness of life does impact how we live in our earthly relationships; but it really has to do with our relationship with the God we cannot see. So there's a balance here of the seen and unseen, and we are called to work hard at both of them.

~ ~ ~ ~ ~

Throughout the centuries, the Church has referred to the work we pursue in our relationship with people and with God through the lens of what's called "the disciplines." The disciplines of the Christian life have been culled out of God's Word and have been used to encapsulate some relational approaches we can both engage in and exhibit abstention in. Although I won't take the time to go over these disciplines in detail, I do want to point you in the right direction.

There are two basic categories of discipline. The first is disciplines of engagement. The second is disciplines of abstention. Disciplines of engagement allow us to work our spiritual muscles. Disciplines of abstention cause us to cease from work and to experience what it means to rest. Taken together, these reflect the beginning of all things. Genesis 1:1–2:3 speaks of how God created (engaged) and how He rested (abstained from creating through Sabbath).

~ ~ ~ ~ ~

Disciplines of engagement include:

- **Study**: seeking to engage God's written and spoken word with a desire to apply it to one's life.

- **Worship**: adoring God both in community with others and privately.

- **Celebration**: taking joy in all the good things our Father has given.

- **Service**: helping others in a time of need in a way that honors God and his creation.

- **Prayer**: conversing with the Lord in a manner that both communicates and listens.

- **Fellowship**: pursuing relationship with other followers of Jesus in contexts like a small group, worship, study, service, etc.

- **Confession**: communicating our sin to God and trusted others in order that forgiveness and victory over sin can be ours.

- **Submission**: coming under the authority of the Lord. This can also be mutual submission within marriage or the community of faith. The purpose is always to direct our efforts to becoming more like Jesus.

Disciplines of abstention include:

- **Solitude**: breaking away from relationships for a specified time to pursue Jesus through prayer or an act of study and worship.

- **Silence**: refraining from speaking for the purpose of being attentive to the Lord.

- **Fasting**: taking a break from eating (or other daily routines) for the purpose of growing in one's hunger for the Lord.

- **Frugality**: choosing to be content with having our common needs met and forsaking the pursuit of comforts and excess.

- **Chastity**: intentionally taking time away from sexual relations with our spouse in order to submit to God's leading rather than physical impulses.

- **Secrecy**: doing for others what Jesus leads us to do without anyone else knowing about it.
- **Sacrifice**: giving up our own efforts toward personal security as we give generously in the name of Jesus.

A fuller explanation of these disciplines can be found in a lot of really good and thorough resources. I'd suggest the following: *The Spirit of the Disciplines* by Dallas Willard; *Celebration of Discipline* by Richard Foster; *The Life You've Always Wanted* by John Ortberg; and *The Workbook on Keeping Company with the Saints* by Maxie Dunnam. It would be well worth our time to pursue understanding these disciplines and applying effort in utilizing them in our lives as the Lord directs.

~ ~ ~ ~ ~

I want to take a quick but important starfish trail right now (an aquatic version of a rabbit trail). I get concerned about how we define growth in godliness, and it's a matter that often weighs people down with unnecessary burdens. When we think of becoming more like Jesus we always think in linear terms: an hour each morning reading the Bible; a half-hour devoted to praying; giving 10 percent of my income at church; saying a word of grace before dinner; etc. But this isn't what the Bible teaches. We each grow in different ways that reflect the uniqueness of who God has made us to be. To underscore this truth, take a moment to digest the following quote:

> Many approaches to spiritual growth assume that the same methods will produce the same growth in different people—but they don't. Because you have been created by God as a unique person, his plan to grow you will not look the same as his plan to grow anyone else. What would grow an orchid would drown a cactus. What would feed a mouse would starve an elephant. All of those entities need light, food, air, and water—but in different amounts and conditions. The key is not treating every creature alike; it is finding the unique conditions that help each creature grow.[2]

Your growth in godliness will not match another person's growth. You might grow best early in the morning by sitting quietly and reading and reflecting on scripture; however, another person may find painting and creating things with their hands to be the place where they experience the presence and wonder of the Lord. You see, we each have a need for unique conditions, and the key is learning what they are and living into them. So don't relegate life with Jesus to simply sitting in a chair and writing thoughts in a journal. For a writer this is a great exercise, but it might be the antithesis of who you are. Figure out what you love to do and pursue it. As you do so, open yourself to God in the midst of those realities and begin to see how God works in you to become who He's made you to be!

On the Other Side of Day 5:

Parable Principle: To pursue something is to take the initiative, because there's something of great value we're after.

Scripture Memory Verse for the Week: *"Let us run with endurance the race God has set before us" (Hebrews 12:1b, NLT).*

Questions for Reflection:

1. Would you agree that the Christian life necessitates personal effort? If so, why? If not, why not?
2. Consider a person you've known who's given effort in their life with Jesus. What was that effort and how did you see the results of it in that person's life?
3. If you could apply one discipline to your life right now, which one would it be and why?
4. What's a unique interest or talent God's given you? Are you taking time to pursue this as a means to growth and working out your salvation?

Taking a Quack at It:

Take some time to study the disciplines more carefully. Prayerfully consider what discipline the Lord might be calling you to take up in this season of your life.

Rescued into a Life of Preparedness

DAY 6: "PREPARED TO RESCUE"

> *15 Look after each other so that none of you fails to receive the grace of God. Watch out that no poisonous root of bitterness grows up to trouble you, corrupting many. 16 Make sure that no one is immoral or godless like Esau, who traded his birthright as the firstborn son for a single meal. 17 You know that afterward, when he wanted his father's blessing, he was rejected. It was too late for repentance, even though he begged with bitter tears.*

On one afternoon in gym class we practiced tag-team wrestling. Mr. Cornick blew his coveted whistle, and we gathered in our corners with our teammates and quickly decided who would take the first turn in the match. Rich was my teammate and, given the fact he was the more adept wrestler, I gave him the choice. After thinking on strategy for a moment or two, Rich decided to have me go in first. If I got into trouble he felt he could rescue me and salvage the match.

So it was agreed. I went in first and within moments I was in the starfish position. Struggling, straining, reaching... I finally hit the flesh of Rich's hand and he came in and won the match! The pendulum swung the other way, and I celebrated the victory as much as Rich did—even though I had done little to garner the victory. I grew to love the strength of a team. It was so much more satisfying than lying in lonely splendor on the vacuum-suctioned reality of my own inabilities.

~ ~ ~ ~ ~

The author of Hebrews is kind of like Mr. Cornick in the sense that he is trying to teach us the value of tag-teams when it comes to whatever wrestling match we're in. Take a moment to think on the following verses: "Look after each other so that none of you fails to receive the grace of God. Watch out that no poisonous root of bitterness grows up to trouble you, corrupting many. Make sure that no one is immoral or godless like Esau, who traded his birthright as the firstborn son for a single meal. You know that afterward, when he wanted his father's blessing, he was rejected. It was too late for repentance, even though he begged with bitter tears" (Hebrews 12:15–17, NLT).

Don't you just love the wording in these verses? Look after... watch out... make sure... These are the words that bring to mind the kinds of things a tag-team expends energy on. Just imagine with me... I'm on my stomach in my starfish position. What's Rich doing? Well, he's looking after where I am in relationship to my opponent (suctioned helplessly to the floor). Rich is watching out for the trajectory of the match (looming ten count). My tag-team teammate is making sure he can help to get me out of the position I'm in and try to salvage the match. This looking after... watching out... and making sure... is the language that makes most sense to the one who's looking to do the rescuing.

Here's the main point: **We have been rescued in order to help rescue**. So all of the preparing we've been studying and focusing on this week culminates in our willingness to help rescue others. "Look after each other so that none of you fails to receive the grace of God" (Hebrews 12:15, NLT). Do you see the expectation? You and I are to look after each other. This is what a tag-team does.

The action of looking after each other implies relationship. For a tag-team to be effective it requires a friendship, trust and relationship between the teammates. The same holds true for us in the Church. We don't look after a stranger and seek to speak into their life without the context of relationship. To do so would cross multiple appropriate and needed boundaries. However, in the context of a trusted and godly relationship where there's been an agreement that accountability can be given and received, looking after each other can become a very healthy and God-honoring reality.

Throughout the ages, the Church has referred to this kind of "looking after" as the "care of souls." We are to care for one another's souls. We are to be intentionally involved in each other's lives with God to such a degree that if it appears a looming ten count may keep us from receiving the grace of God, the other is there to tag in and help swing the match the other way. It's a selfless effort given for the sake of the other.

~ ~ ~ ~ ~

The author of Hebrews goes on to say, "Watch out that no poisonous root of bitterness grows up to trouble you, corrupting many" (Hebrews 12:15b). The role of a tag-team teammate is to keep an eye on the adversary. The teammate may spot something in the opponent that the one in the ring may not be able to see. So it's the strength of having multiple pairs of eyes on the same match that can help to win it. Are we willing to "watch out" for each other? Are we paying close attention to what may be easy to overlook?

Notice how the "root of bitterness" is referred to. Another word for bitterness is "unpleasantness." Note too how a root comes up underfoot and can easily trip up an unsuspecting person. In the language of wrestling, we might call this "foul play" or a "cheap shot." It's the kind of thing the ref may not see that causes one's teammate to go down and lose the match.

So we can think of "roots of bitterness" as those corrupting sins that cause a certain unpleasantness in the life of an individual as well as in the community of faith. They're the selfish and underhanded ways we act that trip us up. They grow underfoot and yet, if we're not aware or mindful, they are the very things that can wind up troubling not just the person in the match, but the whole team as well. "Watch out that no poisonous root of bitterness grows up to trouble you, corrupting many" (Hebrews 12:15b, NLT).

Have you ever been in a local church where you sensed an unpleasantness you couldn't quite put a finger on? Chances are a root of bitterness has been growing for some time and no one's bothered to call it out on the mat. We are to be on the lookout for such things; ready and willing to make sure trouble and corruption don't pin down the life of Christ in you and me.

~ ~ ~ ~ ~

The best kind of teammate is one who "makes sure." They make sure that everyone on the team is where they need to be to garner a win or experience what it means to be a valuable part of the whole. They make sure that no one is left out or on the sidelines feeling unneeded. A true tag-team teammate is one who "makes sure."

The same is true of the Church. We are to "make sure" that no one is headed in a destructive direction. We are to make sure no one is immoral or godless and that everyone in the community knows what it means to be a child of God. The Bible says, "Make sure that no one is immoral or godless like Esau, who traded his birthright as the firstborn son for a single meal. You know that afterward, when he wanted his father's blessing, he was rejected. It was too late for repentance, even though he begged with bitter tears" (Hebrews 12:16–17, NLT).

Look at the progression of what these two verses are saying. Esau was in a favorable position of being the firstborn son with a birthright. But over time and through shoddy actions, he gave up the most valuable reality a man could obtain in that day—all for a single hot meal. Esau traded what was of lasting value for a momentary fix. Isn't this what pins most people down today too? We get hungry for something—love, acceptance, status, respect. We get hungry; and in a moment of time we give up our birthright (children of God) for a momentary fix. But what's this verse really about? Isn't it about the failure of Esau's tag-team teammate? Jacob was there, and he should have been looking after (watching out, making sure) his brother—his teammate, Esau—was winning the match. But he didn't. Jacob gave up being Esau's teammate and actually became the one who pinned down his own brother. He didn't "make sure" and he literally watched his brother go down the road of rejection. Sometimes it's easy to fail at our role of being a tag-teammate. We get tired of looking after, watching out and making sure. But we would do well to be reminded that we are called to be a tag-team with each other. Helping. Tagging in. Sharing the victory. Crying tears of unbelief that we've won rather than weeping because we failed to help rescue and, as a result, our teammate has been defeated.

On the Other Side of Day 6:

Parable Principle: We have been rescued in order to help rescue.

Scripture Memory Verse for the Week: *"Let us run with endurance the race God has set before us" (Hebrews 12:1b, NLT).*

Questions for Reflection:

1. Have you ever teamed up with someone and won a victory? What happened?

2. Have you ever experienced someone looking after, watching out, and making sure you were OK? What did that experience mean to you and why?

3. Would you agree that we are called to help rescue one another? Why or why not?

4. What do you make of the "root of bitterness"? Would you say that the deadliest of sins are those that grow and go unnoticed?

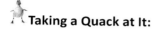**Taking a Quack at It:**

Read the account of Esau and Jacob in Genesis chapters 27–33. Try to study it through the lens of Hebrews 12:15–17. Take some time to consider who is holding you accountable and who you're holding accountable. If there is no accountability in your life, make a determination to become a part of a tag-team.

Day 7: Rest

Worship in community.

Enjoy the presence of loved ones.

Take time to take note of God's creation.

Reflect on this past week.

Commit this coming week to the Lord.

ENDNOTES

1   Amy Carmichael, *Candles in the Dark*, Fort Washington, PA: CLC Publications, 1981, p. 117.

2   John Ortberg, *The Me I Want to Be*. Grand Rapids, MI: Zondervan, 2010, pp. 48–49.

PARABLE 6

W<small>H</small>i<small>TE</small> C<small>A</small><small>N</small>v<small>A</small>s H<small>I</small><small>GH</small> T<small>O</small>ps:
R<small>ESCUED</small> i<small>NTO</small> a L<small>IFE</small> <small>OF</small> C<small>OMMU</small>N<small>I</small>t<small>Y</small>

The noise of lowing cows and snuffling pigs, fuming tractors and cursing hired hands had long since faded for that old barn. So it seemed to welcome some new noise and life. My two older brothers and I responded to the invitation on most afternoons, whether it was blazing hot or freezing cold. I can still remember how we would trek up the steep gravel driveway from our house to the gargantuan front doors of the barn. We'd unlock the padlock and push back the wooden doors. Sunlight would burst into the darkened upstairs recesses, unveiling an open expanse of inexact and uneven floor boards.

We'd take turns sweeping the middle of the floor. We'd carefully remove dust and dirt from the "key," and mark out exactly where the three-point line would be (always a point of endless conflict for three young boys). When the court was finally ready, we would take a quick look at the rusting basketball hoop hanging from the middle rafter to make sure it looked sturdy enough for one more game. In those moments, the smell of old cow manure and the thick air of endlessly rising straw dust would flood into my lungs, and I would be filled with anticipation that we'd have another great matchup.

Bounce. The moment the basketball hit our homemade parquet floor, the sound of fleeing pigeons could be heard in the two silos that were adjoined to the back of the barn. Their cooing and rustling of feathers would mark the start of our endless 1-on-1-on-1. I was always McHale. Matt was Ainge. Mike was Bird.

We'd play for hours and, in our own childlike minds, mimic the moves of the great ones. There might be one lost ball each game (that we'd have to chase after in the bottom of a silo), but we became rather good at basketball. We rehearsed what inspired us. We played out what we longed to be. In it all, we desired to become what was worth becoming: players and a community like the Boston Celtics.

~ ~ ~ ~ ~

The Boston Celtics of the 1980s played the game like they used to play way back when players wore white canvas high tops. The days of Cousy, Pistol Pete Maravich and Chamberlain were the kinds of days when guys didn't showcase themselves or their extravagant footwear. Rather, they blended in with each other and played as a team. They were a community of guys who shared the same passion and lived out the game in tight-knit unity. Sure there were the greats, but even *they* didn't steal the show more than they showcased their teams or offered true classy leadership when the points needed to be made or the passes needed to be given. Teams back then had panache. There was a mystique and a grace to their game. It was the kind of community any young kid dreamed of becoming a part of.

It's different today. Today's basketball is more about the individual. There is no shared sense of community any more. It's not unusual for a star athlete to leave a team if the ability to make a championship is on the line. There's not much loyalty or team spirit. Frankly, it's become boring to watch. I'm tired of the guys who think money and fame is due *them*. How sad to see self-interest take precedence over the needs of the team and the hopes of the ticketholders and local communities. I long for the days when a whole team would work together to make the play and share in the victory. I miss the days when you could count on your team to be there season after season. Back then, I knew when I turned on the TV or the radio that the players I had grown to cherish would be the ones playing the game together. Johnson was certain to make an unbelievable last-minute steal and get it to Bird, who'd put it up for 3. Parrish was the one who'd get the rebound and cherry-pick it to McHale for the inspiring dunk. Bird would throw the no-look pass to Ainge, who'd sink the outside jumper. Those guys were a team. I would have been shocked if Bird had ever donned any other team color or name.

~ ~ ~ ~ ~

Rescued into a Life of Community

Our rescue, obedience, relinquishment, courage and preparedness can all be about our individual selves. Certainly this is what we are most accustomed to in our culture. Even most worship songs have the words "I" and "me" at the center. Yet the culminating work of our Savior is that he didn't go to all the trouble of getting in the thick of the median to carry out just a single duckling. Jesus has rescued the whole lot of us. Salvation is a reality for the plural as much as it is the singular. "We" have been rescued, and once we accept that it's not all about the individual, we begin to see that Jesus has a desire to form us into a team.

The Bible refers to team through the language of community. We are the church community. We are the body. We are the community of faith, formed out of our shared rescue and empowered to live together in unity. We are to be a community attuned to each other's voices but especially sensitive to Jesus'. We need to work together as a team. We need to think of one another. We need to have such a classy act between us that the world will take notice and want to join us to rehearse, enact, mimic… really to become a part of a community where the winsome allure of love and servanthood cannot be easily refused. What this requires is your willingness and my willingness to pull off our fancy footwear that seeks to bring attention to *us*, and to put on white canvas high tops. This humble footwear may not look like much of anything from the outside, but it does remind us on the inside that there are no attention-getting solo acts. Rather, we are a humble community deeply appreciative of each other's talents and gifts, willing to work together to bring all honor and glory to Jesus, who captains our team.

Biblical Text for Week 6: Acts 2:42–47

42 All the believers devoted themselves to the apostles' teaching, and to fellowship, and to sharing in meals (including the Lord's Supper), and to prayer.

43 A deep sense of awe came over them all, and the apostles performed many miraculous signs and wonders. 44 And all the believers met together in one place and shared everything they had. 45 They sold their property and possessions and shared the money with those in need. 46 They worshiped together at the Temple each day, met in homes for the Lord's Supper, and shared their meals with great joy and generosity—47

all the while praising God and enjoying the goodwill of all the people. And each day the Lord added to their fellowship those who were being saved.

Day 1: "Daily Practice"

> 42 All the believers devoted themselves to the apostles' teaching, and to fellowship, and to sharing in meals (including the Lord's Supper), and to prayer.

The biblical passage for this week needs to be looked at as a summary passage. In other words, it's kind of like a menu. You have the usual items for dinner, but there are always nuances, changes and exceptions to the rule. This was the case for the early Church. There was an amalgam of people and situations. There were the good, the bad and the ugly. There were those who didn't give a lick for Jesus or for being a team, and there were those who lived up to the call of Jesus to love God and neighbor. Nevertheless, the normative reality for the early Church is that, on most days and with most believers, they "devoted themselves to the apostles' teaching, and to fellowship, and to sharing in meals (including the Lord's Supper), and to prayer" (Acts 2:42, NLT).

~ ~ ~ ~ ~

For most pastors, there is a rule for church life. Perhaps you've heard of "the 20/80 principle"? Twenty percent of people do all of the work, and 80 percent sit on the bench watching. Well, we may all joke about it, but we loath it when it becomes our reality.

This was the case for me (and it is in some sense for all pastors) when I took a church after my on-campus doctoral program. Now I want to set the context for you. The Beeson Pastor Program at Asbury Seminary was led at the time by Dale Galloway. I attended the program alongside 20 other pastors from all over the world. It was the *Top Gun* of D.Min. opportunities; a chance to travel to the most cutting-edge churches and to learn from the Birds, McHales, Ainges, Parishes and Johnsons of the ministry. We saw massive structures and passionate leadership paradigms. We encountered successful missional programs and unparalleled staff teams. It was an incredible year, and I left the program excited to begin a dynamic path in local church leadership.

About a year after the doctoral program, I remember being outside on a spring afternoon sweating up a storm. Perspiration was flowing down my face... as were tears. I was upset. I was crying because, despite the unavoidable reality of a hayfield growing outside the small church's sanctuary, I couldn't get one person from the church to come over and help mow the lawn. I remember being completely miserable, not because I had to mow (I actually really enjoy the activity), but because I couldn't believe I had gone from learning from the greats to hacking my way through an unsightly church lawn. I remember thinking, *Where are the people of the church? Don't they care?*

~ ~ ~ ~ ~

The local church, if it's to be anything like the church described in Acts 2:42, is to be a place of the all and not just the 20 percent. The church community is to be a team where every last one of us is to be present and involved. "All the believers devoted themselves to the apostles' teaching, and to fellowship, and to sharing in meals (including the Lord's Supper), and to prayer" (Acts 2:42, NLT). What this says to me is that there is a daily practice the early Church took quite seriously. They were devoted to it and made a conscious decision to get off their duffs and participate.

~ ~ ~ ~ ~

Daily practice was the norm for my brothers and me. We went to the upstairs of the barn each and every afternoon because we wanted to become skilled in the game of basketball. Over time, we developed a routine. First we'd stretch and run layups. Next we'd spend time shooting short-range jump shots. As we warmed up, we'd move to the foul line and the 3-point line (invisible, except to us), where we'd take turns drilling downtown shots. We'd practice passing and formations. We were devoted—and underpaid. And here's the cool part: When we played pickup with friends or Tuesday-night basketball at our local church, our efforts showed. We could address the no-look pass because we knew each other's movements and style of play. We made the assists to the right person because we could feel the telltale signs of a hot hand. Playing together became second-nature because we practiced together.

~ ~ ~ ~ ~

Daily practice needs to return to the local church. We need to see that, as a community of believers, once lost and now rescued, we are expected by the Lord of our rescue to become a team through devoted practice with one another. All of us need to know the rhythm of worship, teaching, fellowship, sacraments and prayer through consistent practice. And here's the principle of Acts 2:42: The game is not what counts. What counts are the countless practices—because any teams' ability to win a game is only the natural outcome of having worked hard together in practice. We need to reverse our understanding because, in a real sense, the practice is the game and the game is the result of the practice.

Putting this in local-church and community language, I'm saying that our ability to serve each other in love is the result of getting to know each other in fellowship. Our adeptness in service is the result of gathering around the table of the Lord and being reminded that true servanthood is the laying down of one's life for another. Our skill at handling the tough circumstances of life is the direct outcome of praying together for one another and the needs of the world. Our selfless humility stems from the willingness to take in and meditate on the teachings of scripture. In other words, if we are not in daily practice, the longing to be a God-honoring team will never come to pass.

Another element of Acts 2:42 which needs rehearsing in our minds, is the devotion of the "all." I think we've lost this in the local church, but its meaning is significant. **All of us are accountable to all of us**. Think of the Boston Celtics for a moment. Imagine if Larry Bird had never showed up for practice. It would have impacted the whole team, wouldn't it? Or think for a moment of Robert Parish quitting practice mid-way. The ability to work with McHale and Bird on rebounds would have suffered. So too our decision to not stay devoted affects the whole church. When I'm not in fellowship or worship—when I refrain from meditating on God's word or praying—I am, in a very real sense, contributing to the perspiration and tears of the other persons on my team. My lack of devotion contributes to the overabundance of loneliness and despair felt throughout the team of my local church. I am culpable in my team's inability to win.

~ ~ ~ ~ ~

It had been over a year since I had talked with my colleague in ministry. He had been leading a church close to mine but had moved to take another local church. It was at an Annual Conference that I finally caught up with him and asked how things were going at his new church. A big smile grew over his face. I was interested.

> "Tim. The most amazing thing has happened in my church this past year. When I got there it had been on a plateau for decades. Pastors had come and gone, and it was a meat-grinder for ministers. When I went I was really scared about becoming another statistic in the church's long line of local pastors. But then something unexpected happened. We had a special week of revival services, and on one of the evenings Bill interrupted the service and came forward to share something important with the church. He was a gruff and angry man, so I was concerned about what might come out of his mouth. He had been a member of the church for decades and caused more pain than good. But he had to fight back the tears as he shared with the church how he had asked Jesus to forgive his hardness of heart. He told all of us how sorry he was for his stingy leadership that never allowed the church to change and grow. He asked for our forgiveness and, I've gotta tell you, from that night on the church has been exploding with people! It's like the whole community turned the corner after Bill shared. Person after person came forward and began to cry and make restitution with those they had wronged. I've never seen anything like it."

I'll never forget hearing that story. One person had deliberately chosen not to come to practice for decades. But Jesus changed his heart and, when Bill got right with the Lord and his team, the whole church turned a corner. What about you? Have you been choosing not to practice with your team? If so, do you think opening your heart to becoming a part of the "all" might change things?

On the Other Side of Day 1:

Parable Principle: All of us are accountable to all of us.

Scripture Memory Verse for the Week: *"All of you should be of one mind. Sympathize with each other. Love each other as brothers and sisters. Be tenderhearted, and keep a humble attitude"* (1 Peter 3:8, NLT).

Questions for Reflection:

1. In what area of your life has daily practice helped you become successful?
2. Have you ever practiced with a team? If so, what are some learnings you made in the process?
3. Do you agree that all of us are accountable to the all in the local church? Why or why not?
4. How have you contributed in a positive way to the health of the church community? Are there ways in which you have failed to be present? How has this hurt your church community? Why have you chosen not to show up for practice?
5. Have you ever witnessed a story like Bill's? What happened? How did it bring healing to the church?
6. What is the Lord calling you to practice in the here and now?

Taking a Quack at It:

Take the initiative to learn from your church leadership what the needs of the community are. Pray over what practices the Lord would have you become devoted to. Make the commitment and calendar it.

Day 2: "Awe"

> 43 A deep sense of awe came over them all, and the apostles performed many miraculous signs and wonders.

I love the "awe" moments in the game of basketball. Those occasions when a shot is made or a dunk is thrown down that just simply defies all odds. I remember watching Larry Bird play the Portland Trailblazers on February 14, 1986. It was an awe-inspiring game where Bird had 47 points, 11 assists and 14 rebounds. And, get this: 22 of the points were made off of his left hand! (He was right handed.) The Celtics won in overtime. As a 14-year-old, I was left spellbound. In that game I learned that awe can be a good thing. It can create a sense of reverence for the players and can help a kid develop team loyalty.

~ ~ ~ ~ ~

The early Church had some awe moments, too. "A deep sense of awe came over them all, and the apostles performed many miraculous signs and wonders" (Acts 2:43, NLT). It's interesting that the word for "awe" literally means "fear." So we could translate this same verse in the following way: "A deep sense of fear came over them all." Now we have to pay attention to the reason for the awe (another good word is "reverence"). It was not to draw the Church to a fanfare kind of approach towards the Apostles. In other words, the community of believers didn't have posters of the Apostles up on their walls or trading cards in their pockets; rather, all of the people, including the Apostles, experienced awe for the purpose of worshiping the one true God (cf. Acts 2:47a).

~ ~ ~ ~ ~

Whether we're the Church of the first century or the twenty-first century, our tendency to commit idolatry remains. I see this all the time in church ministry. A pastor is idolized. A staff person is put on a pedestal. A particular speaker or leader is lauded. Such idolatry is often subtle in nature. We don't mean for it to happen. We certainly don't intend to worship the creature rather than the Creator. But, over time, and if we're not cautious, we can easily confuse fear of the Lord with awe over the people God uses.

I believe it's this proneness to idolize that caused the Lord to make the sin of idolatry the very first topic of conversation on Mt. Sinai with Moses. Just take a moment to recall the 10 Commandments. The very first one is, "You must not have any other god but me" (Exodus 20:3, NLT). God knows who we are and what we're capable of. He understands the very first step we yearn to take outside of his will is to have a multiplicity of gods. This is a part of being made for worship. God created us to worship, and this innate need of ours often shows itself in a desire to worship those who can throw down 22 points off of their left hand. You see, in our awe, we tend to stop short of the Lord we cannot see and worship the ones we can see.

The early Church fell into this sin time and time again. They'd latch onto an Apostle and begin to idolize the person rather than the Lord. Yet the Apostles were adept at countering what could have easily become fanfare. They didn't allow it for a second. (If you'd like to take a look at one such instance, refer to 1 Corinthians 1:10–17.) Suffice it to say this passage reflects Paul's willingness to be weak in public speech in order that the cross of Christ would not lose its power. Simply put, Paul avoided self-promotion in order to point people to the message of the cross and worship of Christ Jesus.

~ ~ ~ ~

One of the areas of community life we have to own and confess is our tendency to become fans of people rather than worshippers of the Lord. The direct result of panting after an awe-inspiring preacher or leader is the constant movement of people from one church to another. Loyalty to a community of faith has been replaced by idolization of the ministry leaders or talents of the people at the "church down the road." God help us! He intended the awe we experience in our local community to draw us closer to him and closer to each other. My prayer is that we'll see more leaders in local churches who are willing to humble themselves and glory in their weaknesses. I also pray we'll see a rapid diminishment of ego-centered ministry leaders who travel the conference circuits in order to hear more applause and garner more posters and trading cards.

ON THE OTHER SIDE OF DAY 2:

Parable Principle: One of the areas of community life we have to own and confess is our tendency to become fans of people rather than worshippers of the Lord.

Scripture Memory Verse: "All of you should be of one mind. Sympathize with each other. Love each other as brothers and sisters. Be tenderhearted, and keep a humble attitude" (1 Peter 3:8, NLT).

Questions for Reflection:

1. What are some memorable "awe" moments in your life? What memory do they leave with you?

2. Do you agree we tend to commit idolatry? Why or why not?

3. What are some ways the local church can seek to guard against idolatry?

4. Who do you know that's remained faithful to their local church throughout the years? What lessons can their "team loyalty" teach you?

5. In what way are you remaining close to Jesus and ridding your life of idols?

Taking a Quack at It:

Take some time to read 1 Corinthians 1:10–17. Zero in on 1 Corinthians 1:17. How does our own cleverness diminish the power of the cross? How might this be true in your life?

Day 3: "Making the Assist"

> *44 And all the believers met together in one place and shared everything they had. 45 They sold their property and possessions and shared the money with those in need.*

A good basketball team is known for making good assists. Likewise, a great basketball player is known for his willingness to offer to another teammate the opportunity to score the points. Consistent assists simply reflect the core conviction of a community of players: that the team is more important than the individual.

Larry Bird was a great assist-maker. Magic Johnson was showier than Bird, but both of them were known for their ability to make the assist. Without the assists, neither Bird nor Johnson would have garnered the amount of triple-doubles they did in the seasons they played.

A player's ability to make the assist has to do with the posture and attitude of mind that they take into the game. It's a mindset of being willing to hold the ball loosely because someone else might be able to take and make the best shot. In other words, ball hogs will disable a team's ability to be known for assists and for being a well-functioning team where every player has the opportunity to be applauded and appreciated.

~ ~ ~ ~ ~

Tim Schmitt was probably one of the best players I ever got to play the game of basketball with. Although he was more than a decade older than me, he had played basketball consistently since grade school. I first met Tim at Tuesday night basketball games at the Owego Church of the Nazarene. Guys would leave work, get dinner in the local drive-thru, and come to church where the gym would be open and the lights would be flickering a fluorescent glow. Tim was always there first. He had the key to the gym and was the one who spearheaded the activity.

Tim was known for making the assist. He could shoot the ball better than the rest of us, but he could also make the kind of passes that left you batting at thin air on defense. It took everything to follow his hands. *Where'd the ball go?* This was a constant refrain in my mind whenever I played against Tim. What was cool to experience was the change in me and my understanding of the game. When I had first come to those Tuesday night pickup games, I had arrived with dreams of making the 3-pointers and nailing the short jump shots. What I began to understand was the value of a good pass that got the ball out of one person's hands and into another's. With a play like that, two people rather than one shared the fun of making the points for the good of the team. The win was distributed to a larger group of players.

~ ~ ~ ~

Acts 2:44–45 says, "And all the believers met together in one place and shared everything they had. They sold their property and possessions and shared the money with those in need." What these verses tell us is that the early Church knew how to make the assist. They met together and they shared everything. If they needed to, they held possessions loosely and shared the proceeds with people who required assistance. Now remember, there was no welfare system. There were no government-run programs or agencies. The burden for caring for one another's very real needs was shared by the community of the local church.

Making the assist—or in this case, sharing—is not easy to do. That's why, from a very young age, we cry over having to share a toy with a playmate or a cookie with a sibling. We don't like to share. We tend to be ball hogs. We like to hold onto things and claim them, even in the face of the needs of others. But the Lord has called the Church to be a community that makes the assist.

~ ~ ~ ~ ~

Rescued into a Life of Community

One of the most beautiful assists I've ever received was when I helped lead a summertime VBS. We had more than 100 children coming to our small church for Vacation Bible School, but had no idea how we were going to get the resources that would support the week's event. All of that changed when I called a nearby local church that was known for the fantastic kind of VBS they put on each year. The church had several stage hands who worked with professional props. They could take a large sheet of Styrofoam and make it look like the side of Montezuma's temple. It turned out their VBS was just a couple of weeks prior to ours. When I told them of our need for any kind of themed props they might have left when they were done, they graciously said we could take all of theirs to our church, for free!

I remember my father-in-law's face when we drove over a U-Haul to pick up the items. We couldn't believe the Aztec volcano (working, no less) and the temple walls. We couldn't get over the palm trees and the scenic vegetation. The handcrafted wildlife and foliage were on par with what you might find at a Disney theme park. We were blown away. Needless to say, when the children arrived for VBS, they were shocked by the setup. At each day's end the kids wanted to stay. They felt like they were in another world. That local church's generosity met a palpable need, and it took the talent of their community and expanded the influence of love and support into our community. They held their resources loosely, and we became beneficiaries. I bet those kids (now mostly grown) still vividly remember that summer's VBS.

~ ~ ~ ~ ~

Making the assist is something all of us can become proficient at. Each day there are numerous opportunities to share with those in need. Sometimes the need might be for a family to receive dinner while a father or a mother goes through medical treatments. Other times the need might be for a group leader at the summer VBS or a small-group facilitator at a weekly Bible study. There might be a neighbor who could use help with mowing the lawn or a local food pantry in need of helpers to organize canned goods. Making the assist and expanding the Church's influence in the community pleases God. It also teaches us that generosity and a loose grip keep the Church functioning like a healthy team, and help each person learn that **giving and not simply taking cultivates the mind of a Jesus follower.**

ON THE OTHER SIDE OF DAY 3:

Parable Principle: Giving and not simply taking cultivates the mind of a Jesus follower.

Scripture Memory Verse: *"All of you should be of one mind. Sympathize with each other. Love each other as brothers and sisters. Be tenderhearted, and keep a humble attitude"* (1 Peter 3:8, NLT).

Questions for Reflection:

1. Have you ever received something from another person that changed your circumstances for the better? How did that gift impact and change you?

2. As you reflect on your experience in the community of Jesus, what are some ways you've witnessed the Church making the assist? Are their times you've felt the church community has held onto things too tightly? Why was that the case?

3. Name one time when you invested in someone else's life and made a loving impact. How did that experience affect you? Why?

Taking a Quack at It:

John Wesley is quoted as saying, "Make all you can. Save all you can. Give all you can." It's been said early Methodism tended to live by the first two statements but failed in third: giving. The church grew quite wealthy as a result. Yet John Wesley himself lived in such a way that, when he died, he lacked the ability to rub two pennies together. He left basically nothing of monetary value behind. He had given everything away.

What are you holding onto tightly? Ponder and pray over this question. The truth is that anything we hold tight-fisted may very well be an idol. God wants nothing to stand between you and Him. So what do you need to let go of? What do you need to take a loose grip on? What do you need to give away? Make the decision to do so today.

Day 4: "Parquet Floor"

> *46 They worshiped together at the Temple each day, met in homes for the Lord's Supper, and shared their meals with great joy and generosity.*

Throughout the National Basketball Association, the original Boston Garden was known to have the most unusual court surface. It was a parquet floor, made up of uneven floor boards and dead spots where a normal bouncing ball could fall flat. The Celtics knew the court knew intimately well. The players knew the contours of the floor and how to navigate effectively on it. Opponents had a different reality. Players might trip or lose a certain sense of equilibrium and comfort. Balls might unexpectedly go out of bounds, or a bounce pass might not go in the intended direction or distance. It took skill and practice to play well on the Boston Garden's parquet floor.

My brothers and I had our own parquet floor in the upstairs of our grandfather's barn. Wooden floor boards in an old barn are not built for smoothness sake. There is no architectural conviction that the floor is meant to respond to the bounce of a Wilson ball. My brothers and I had to learn to navigate that rough and uneven floor. We had to practice on it and gain insight into where to bounce the ball and how to pass and dribble. We always believed that this court was our own humble version of the Boston Garden.

~ ~ ~ ~ ~

The early Church was like the Boston Garden's parquet floor. It was unique. It was filled with dynamic and changing contours. It was a rarity. Luke, the author of Acts, recounts, "They worshipped together at the Temple each day, met in homes for the Lord's Supper and shared their meals with great joy and generosity" (Acts 2:46, NLT). Notice the variances of community life. There was worship on a daily basis, but it didn't end there. Community members also gathered in various homes for the purpose of sharing meals, as well as the Lord's Supper. Joy marked their gatherings and, when there was a need, the community was predisposed to being generous with one another. In other words, you never knew what you might experience in the church from day to day.

~ ~ ~ ~ ~

I often get a sense that one of two things typically happen in local churches today. More often than not the majority of people believe church is about the building where they gather one hour a week for worship. This is kind of like a shopping-mall mentality, where a group of strangers converge in lobbies and sanctuaries all over the country to sing and hear the Word of God. After about 60 minutes, the people head out the doors and won't encounter the community for another seven days.

The second approach is that worship is followed by a one-size-fits-all opportunity for adults to grow in spiritual formation. Typically the growth aspect is another hour-long venue in the church's building, where people gather in smaller groups for the purpose of studying God's Word. This simple approach seeks to streamline things and make church life easy and convenient. People may begin to get to know some other people, but the format tends to make spiritual formation a stunted experience of growing mostly in head knowledge.

The example of early Church counters our tendency to create a smooth-home-court approach to life in Jesus. Members of the early Church had quite the parquet-floor experience, and they learned to navigate the nuances with skill and precision. Just imagine. The book of Acts says they worshipped daily at the Temple. The word "daily" implies a consistent commitment on the part of the church to be in community with one another. They were committed to gathering together in worship, and their Jewish context of Temple meant they were not only Jewish Christians but also believers who gathered in the center of the local community (the Temple). So these men and women, young and old alike, were growing in relationship with the Lord AND one another AND the community—on a consistent, daily basis. Their experience had a lot of contours to it.

Members of the early Church also met in homes. The people went from the more formal worship in a set-apart setting (the Temple) to a more informal setting of a family's home and it's generous hospitality. I've always found that welcoming people into our home is a humbling reality. The house is not always pristine and perfect. Not only do people see who we really are, but they also get a sense of the kind of life we lead. Throughout the house, Tracey's photos of the kids, family and friends reflect our love of relationship and our value of family. Our books, games, movies, food and more all tell a story of who we are when we're not pressed and ironed and neatly presented outside of the house. Gathering in the home creates a completely unique environment for the community of the church that a church building cannot offer.

Members of the early Church also practiced the sacraments in their gatherings at the homes. How often do we intentionally gather in a house to grow deeper in relationship with one another and to receive a means of grace? That's what a sacrament is, after all. It's a means of grace; a literal way in which we experience God's palpable love and mercy. How intimate! How unique! How needed! This is formation in Jesus, and it is experienced in the humble welcome of a family receiving others in for the purpose of growth in Jesus.

Acts chapter 2 goes on to say that the people shared meals together with "great joy and generosity" (Acts 2:46b, NLT). The best cuts of beef, the most delectable of fruits, the finest breads were generously offered and received as people gathered together. They weren't meeting over bulk-rate franks or stale baguettes; the people of the church put out their best in order to honor the guests who had stepped onto their home courts.

When I offer my best to another person, something happens in my heart. I begin to change. I start to feel something deeper for the other person that wouldn't have stirred up in me otherwise. You see, when we truly honor another person, we start to think more highly of them. When we tangibly invest in another person, we begin to believe in who God has made them to be. When we offer the best, we begin to think the best of the other person.

I think churches that suffer from belittling each other and gossiping about one another are communities of people that have never taken a hold of accounts like these in God's Word. They've missed something of what it means to be a community that approaches life together in as unique and creative a way as a patched-together parquet floor. They may be communities that meet for formal worship, but more than likely they are not places of worship where people also open their homes, offer their best and, in offering their best, begin to approach each other with the best in mind.

Acts 2:46 reminds us that we have an opportunity to move past convenient approaches to community that may look neat and wrinkle-free on paper but lack the nuances and creative variances that can make a group of people a church. In order to become the people God has called us to be, we have to navigate together, with purpose and skill, over the parquet of worship, relationship, sacrament, joy and generosity. When we do so, there's something wonderfully rare that happens: We become a distinct community of people that actually honors Jesus through our worship and honors one another with our time and our best.

ON THE OTHER SIDE OF DAY 4:

Parable Principle: The example of the early Church counters our tendency to create a smooth-home-court approach to life in Jesus.

Scripture Memory Verse: *"All of you should be of one mind. Sympathize with each other. Love each other as brothers and sisters. Be tenderhearted, and keep a humble attitude"* (1 Peter 3:8, NLT).

Questions for Reflection:

1. Define what church means to you, in terms of your actual practices.

2. What are the most meaningful aspects of church life to you? Why?

3. The early Church practiced a variety of approaches to worship and community life. How are these practices similar to, or different from, what most local churches practice today?

4. Think of an occasion when generous hospitality was offered to you. What was the experience like? How did it shape you and your relationship with the person(s) who opened their home?

5. Do you agree that offering our best to another person changes the way we view and relate to that other person? Why or why not?

Taking a Quack at It:

Make an intentional effort to be present at your church's next celebration of the Lord's Supper. As you receive the broken body and shed blood of Jesus, ponder what this means for you and your church's community. How could the best that Jesus offered nourish the community in how they worship God and relate to one another? As Jesus welcomes you to receive what he has generously given on the cross, be open to how he might want you to generously give out of love to someone else.

Day 5: "Home-Court Advantage"

> *47 ...All the while praising God and enjoying the goodwill of all the people.*

I used to love it when the Celtics had their backs against the wall in a seven-game series, and the championship had come down to the final tooth-and-nail game. The hair on the back of my neck used to stand on end as the home-court fans in Boston Garden would stand and cheer, hoot and holler, clap and wave their shirts, trinkets and souvenir purchases. It always seemed that the home-court advantage gave the beleaguered Celtics an edge and a hope, no matter how many points they might be down. And then the unthinkable would happen—a stolen ball, a no-look pass, an amazing 3-pointer, an incredible win. The stands would empty, and the fans would go wild! I was mesmerized by the home-court advantage and, if I had had the money, I would have travelled the eight hours from Lounsberry, New York to the inner-city of Boston and been a part of the home-court advantage.

~ ~ ~ ~ ~

The early Church experienced the home-court advantage, according to the author of Acts. "They worshipped together at the Temple each day, met in homes for the Lord's Supper, and shared their meals with great joy and generosity—all the while praising God and enjoying the goodwill of all the people" (Acts 2:46–47a, NLT). Take a moment to ponder what it means that the church experienced the goodwill of all the people.

The marketplace is glutted with resources and books that seem to pit the church against the world. I've heard people say that we need to become "barbarian Christians"—warriors and terrifying harbingers of destruction on par with an Old Testament sword-wielding prophet. Now don't get me wrong. I certainly believe we need to be courageous in this world (week 4 tackled this subject), but I also believe the church has lost touch with the call to be peaceable, compassionate, kind, gentle... and dare I say, nice?

The Apostle Paul counseled the Church in Rome saying, "Bless those who persecute you. Don't curse them; pray that God will bless them. Be happy with those who are happy, and weep with those who weep. Live in harmony with each other. Don't be too proud to enjoy the company of ordinary people. And don't think you know it all! Never pay back evil with more evil. Do things in such a way that everyone can see you are honorable. Do all you can to live in peace with everyone" (Romans 12:14–18, NLT). This teaching of Paul makes me think of Jesus when he stood before pompous Pilate. The Bible says Jesus was like a lamb before the slaughter who uttered not a single word of insult, anger or condemnation. He humbly endured the suffering and the cross, and exhibited an honorable godliness through it all.

I guess this is why I shudder when I hear present-day church leaders proclaim that we are called to be shield-toting Vikings. Do we really want to be styled as barbaric? I mean, really. Does a barbarian never pay back evil? Does a barbarian live at peace with everyone? Does a barbarian pray for his enemies? Of course not! A barbarian plunders, kills, maims and strikes fear and terror into the hearts of people. This is not the call of Jesus Christ. We are called to live at peace and to show, through the example of our lives, that we love like Jesus loved.

Paul counsels his young associate, Timothy, along similar lines when he instructs, "I urge you, first of all, to pray for all people. Ask God to help them; intercede on their behalf, and give thanks for them. Pray this way for kings and all who are in authority so that we can live peaceful and quiet lives marked by godliness and dignity. This is good and pleases God our Savior, who wants everyone to be saved and to understand the truth" (1 Timothy 2:1–4, NLT). What Paul is saying is that the most effective way to evangelize the world is to love the world. We don't do any justice to our Lord of compassion and forgiveness if we're gnashing our teeth and striking out at the world around us with condescension and arrogance.

~ ~ ~ ~ ~

I had just gotten out of work and was heading to the grocery store to pick up last-minute items for dinner when I spotted a young woman sitting in her car that had stalled by the grocery store curb. With only one glance, I could see that she was on the phone pleading for help. She was crying. Nevertheless, I was busy. It had been a long day, and I just wanted to get home to Tracey and the kids. So I drove past the young woman and thought, *I'm sure someone else will stop and help her out.*

Several minutes later I left the checkout area and headed to my car. I looked over to where the woman had been stranded moments before and, sure enough, she was still there and still alone. I continued toward my car. *Boundaries, Tim! Don't worry about her. Someone's definitely on their way to help.* I drove past her and tried to get on with the early evening, but something nagged me on the inside. It was the Lord. He made it abundantly clear that I needed to turn around and help. *Darn it, God! I have no desire to be the Good Samaritan!* Guilt flooded me. My evening was about to stall out if I didn't respond with obedience. So about a quarter of mile up the street I did a u-turn and headed back, loathing the interruption. When I got there, the high-school student was still stranded and still alone. Cars simply made an arc around her unintentional obstruction near the grocery store.

I parked my car and walked up to the passenger-side window. Bowing low so I could be seen by her, I asked if she needed help. No words came out—just tears and a helpless nod or two of her head. I told her to put her car in neutral and I pushed her compact car into the nearest empty parking space. I asked what the trouble was, and she said, "I ran out of gas." So I ran back into the grocery store, bought a small gas container, walked over to the gas station next door, filled it up and poured it into her gas tank. The car started without a hiccup.

Profuse thanks and gratitude came toward me. I simply said, "No problem; I hope you have a great day!"

I was walking back to my car when I was encountered by a college-aged man. He said, "Hey sir! I've been watching what you did for that girl over there, and I just wanted to say thanks. It really means a lot to me that you'd help her out. It's really cool." I smiled and thanked him, but told him it had not been too much of an effort.

What struck me as I got back into my car was that I had actually been used by God to speak into the heart of a young man who happened to take notice of an inconvenience God had prompted me to respond to. So here's the lesson: **How we live in the interruptions speaks volumes to the people who are watching what we do with a hurting world.**

~ ~ ~ ~ ~

Just like the young man who thanked me, the early Church received the goodwill of all the people who were eyeing the way they lived. They gained a home-court advantage, not because they snarled and shook their fists at the world around them, but because they lived peaceable lives of love and prayer that communicated deep kindness and compassion. It's been said that people may doubt what you say, but they will believe what you do. The early Church did acts of love and goodness. The early Church prayed for their enemies and blessed those who persecuted them. The early church, in so doing, reaped exactly what they sowed: The goodwill of all the people. The home-court advantage. We would do well to do the same today.

ON THE OTHER SIDE OF DAY 5:

Parable Principle: How we live in the interruptions speaks volumes to the people who are watching what we do with a hurting world.

Scripture Memory Verse: *"All of you should be of one mind. Sympathize with each other. Love each other as brothers and sisters. Be tenderhearted, and keep a humble attitude" (1 Peter 3:8, NLT).*

Questions for Reflection:

1. Have you ever been to a sporting event where you were a part of the home-court advantage? What was that experience like? What did it make you think and feel?

2. In what ways has your church garnered the goodwill of the people in the community? Why?

3. How could the church impact the community to such a degree that people can't help but take notice of the love and kindness being shown?

4. What areas of your personal life are quiet and peaceable?

5. Who would your neighbors say you are, based on their experience of you and your family?

Taking a Quack at It:

Make a decision to respond to the people around you with kindness and compassion. Ask the Lord to help you exhibit godliness and a deep sense of dignity. When interruptions come your way, respond immediately with obedience.

DAY 6: "WALK-ONS WELCOME"

> 47 And each day the Lord added to their fellowship those who were being saved.

Famous stories of walk-ons are a part of our American cultural storytelling. We gain a lot of powerful emotion from recounting these kinds of events, and parents love to use such legends as opportunities to instill perseverance and courage in their children. Take the movie *Rudy* as an example. This box-office sensation tells the story of a young man who had always been told he was way too small to play football for his favorite team, the Fighting Irish. Rudy is a true underdog in this 1993 film directed by David Anspaugh, and movie-goers cried, cheered and left the film ready to tackle (no pun intended) their own insurmountable realities.

Although walk-ons used to be allowed in sports, that practice has been abandoned. Accounts like Rudy's incredible journey no longer happen. Walk-ons are a thing of history in sports. It's a sad reality, but it's true. Today's athletes need agents, records and longstanding histories of playing sports successfully to even have a chance of trying out for a team.

~ ~ ~ ~ ~

The unfortunate disappearance of walk-ons is not simply a sad tale in present-day sports; it's also a problem for the local church. More often than not, local churches do not welcome walk-ons. We resist new people coming into our churches. We don't like having to make new relationships or to open up our small groups or worship services to new people. We love what we're used to and, although we might give a gift or a handshake, we often go back to our team and run the same plays at church with the same people week in and week out.

The early Church, maybe even out of necessity, loved walk-ons. "And each day the Lord added to their fellowship those who were being saved" (Acts 2:47b). Now before you move on and imagine this to be an insignificant collection of words, take time to think about what is being said. *Every day* the Lord added new people who were being saved. This means a lot of new relationships had to be made, room in the homes had to be expanded, and openness to daily change became the norm. It means that the early Church was flexible and approachable. Outsiders felt comfortable becoming a part of the team.

~ ~ ~ ~

The teen ministry that blossomed and grew at our church in Boston was a place where a constant reception of walk-ons took place. Our youth pastor reached out lovingly, and the teens in the community responded. I've gotta tell you, it wasn't always easy for me. The names were hard to pronounce. The cultures represented were in many ways similar but also quite different from my own experience. Over time the downstairs part of the church, that had once housed a preschool, now had to make room for a massive group of teens on Sunday morning. Couches, posters, overstuffed chairs, Bibles and teenage décor sprouted overnight and filled the small space to overflowing.

I remember sometimes feeling like I had to apologize for the change in the church space and the walk-ons who kept streaming into the church each week. Some of the church-goers didn't like the cigarette butts strewn outside the front doors. Others were quite upset when the teens would roughhouse and the drywall would take the brunt of the matches. Constant spackling and cleanup didn't help matters. But there was a growing core of us at the church that began to take ownership of the Lord's call to be a church where walk-ons were welcome. Although it wasn't always easy, I know it pleased the Lord.

~ ~ ~ ~

I want you to catch this point in the book of Acts. The early Church (on average) was an environment where there was daily commitment to the life of Jesus (see day 1 of this week), there was a sense of awe at the work of the Lord (see day 2), there was a spirit of generosity and teamwork (see day 3), there was a community with a lot of nuance and investment going on (see day 4), and there was goodwill and appreciation of their loving presence by those outside the church (cf. day 5). All of this worked together to create an environment and milieu where walk-ons would be a natural result.

Who did the adding of walk-ons? The pastor? The committee on evangelism? The missional passions of a core group of members? Well, indirectly maybe. But actually it was the Lord. "The Lord added to their fellowship" (Acts 2:47, NLT).

Here's the simple and plain truth: The Lord will add walk-ons if we are committed to living the life of Jesus as a community... as a team. If a local church is not adding walk-ons, there's a pretty good chance a breakdown has happened somewhere in community life and somewhere in obedience to the Lord. In other words, those who might seek to walk-on—with all of the courage and discomfort that might entail—simply don't, because they're getting a message that walk-ons aren't welcome. The Lord calls us to reassess and reevaluate whether we are open to new faces, names, backgrounds and cultures. Further, he seeks to find out if we are willing to open ourselves to the Lord's additions to our fellowship for the purpose of salvation. Can having walk-ons become a daily reality and not a thing of legend—a good tearjerker story of the past that just simply doesn't happen anymore?

ON THE OTHER SIDE OF DAY 6:

Parable Principle: The early Church, maybe even out of necessity, loved walk-ons.

Scripture Memory Verse: *"All of you should be of one mind. Sympathize with each other. Love each other as brothers and sisters. Be tenderhearted, and keep a humble attitude"* (1 Peter 3:8, NLT).

Questions for Reflection:

1. What account of a walk-on has spoken to you powerfully in the past? What were you encouraged to do as a result of learning about the determination of that person?

2. Do you agree or disagree that the local church tends to be unwelcoming to walk-ons? Why?

3. What would need to happen in your life for you to become flexible enough to welcome walk-ons?

4. What are some changes that would need to take place in your local church for you to become a place where the Lord can add daily those who are being saved?

5. How are we to rely on the Lord to do the adding? What might this look like?

Taking a Quack at It:

Read Matthew 9:35–38. Follow what Jesus instructs in this passage.

Day 7: Rest

Worship in community.

Enjoy the presence of loved ones.

Take time to take note of God's creation.

Reflect on this past week.

Commit this coming week to the Lord.

Conclusion

This six-week study is simply an exercise to help us stop and rethink how we're living on the other side of our rescue. God has rescued us and has called us into a particular kind of life. This isn't a one-time, "I-got-saved!" experience. This is a lifetime walk of intentionally choosing to exhibit gratitude for all the Lord has done. This is a daily obedience to particular teachings and commands Jesus has given us. This is the willingness (reluctant at times) to relinquish life as we once knew it and journey into the shadow of the cross. This is a life of courageously standing for Jesus in the midst of darkness and pain. This is the ongoing preparation we take on, to be the hands and (webbed) feet of Jesus as we accept our needed place in the life of the Church. You and I are the Church. Further, you and I are saints; and I pray that this short pause has provided your webbed feet both a springboard to propel you forward and a respite to be encouraged and reminded of what an awesome privilege it is to be called a Christian.